MW00436145

Reverend Kelley's work is ˙God-sent ˑˑ for the church. It helps to show the liberating truth of the gospel; it also opens your vision to see the manipulative effects of living by "works." The case studies are very distinguishing in assisting you to practically see the freedom of the gospel and the danger of exchanging works for the reality of the gospel of God in Jesus Christ. It is God's blessing for all of us. Thank you, Reverend Kelley.

—REV. DR. ISAIAH JONES JR.
SENIOR PASTOR, COVENANT PRESBYTERIAN CHURCH
PALO ALTO, CA
MODERATOR, THE PRESBYTERY OF SAN JOSE
WRITER OF THE GOSPEL CLASSIC "GOD HAS SMILED ON ME"

Men of the cloth have attempted to establish their ideal of holiness through doctrine of men and the tradition of the elders, which have made the Word of God of non-effect. Lorretta has shed the light of grace and truth to expose the darkness of men's religion. The truth makes us free.

—REV. A. J. MAGGOS
SENIOR PASTOR, OPEN DOOR FELLOWSHIP
PRESIDENT, OPEN DOOR MINISTRIES, ALTON, IL

Reverend Kelley shares how practical Christian living can be balanced with spiritual truth. The plague of legalism has held people in bondage for years. Insights and revelations in this book have exposed the angel of light. Galatians 5:1 instructs us to "stand fast therefore in the liberty wherewith Christ hath made us free, and be not entangled again with the yolk of bondage."

—REV. THOMAS E. BRANHAM
INDIANA DISTRICT BISHOP AND ASSISTANT GENERAL BISHOP
NORTHEASTERN DIVISION
PENTECOSTAL CHURCH OF GOD

BALANCE
OR
BONDAGE

BALANCE OR BONDAGE

Lorretta Kelley

CREATION
HOUSE
A STRANG COMPANY

BALANCE OR BONDAGE by Lorretta Kelley
Published by Creation House
A Strang Company
600 Rinehart Road
Lake Mary, Florida 32746
www.creationhouse.com

This book or parts thereof may not be reproduced in any form, stored in a retrieval system, or transmitted in any form by any means—electronic, mechanical, photocopy, recording, or otherwise—without prior written permission of the publisher, except as provided by United States of America copyright law.

Unless otherwise noted, all Scripture quotations are from the King James Version of the Bible.

Scripture quotations marked AMP are from the Amplified Bible. Old Testament copyright © 1965, 1987 by the Zondervan Corporation. The Amplified New Testament copyright © 1954, 1958, 1987 by the Lockman Foundation. Used by permission.

Scripture quotations marked CEV are from the Contemporary English Version, copyright © 1995 by the American Bible Society. Used by permission.

Scripture quotations marked NKJV are from the New King James Version of the Bible. Copyright © 1979, 1980, 1982 by Thomas Nelson, Inc., publishers. Used by permission.

Scripture quotations marked NLT are from the Holy Bible, New Living Translation, copyright © 1996. Used by permission of Tyndale House Publishers, Inc., Wheaton, IL 60189. All rights reserved.

Greek word definitions are taken from *Strong's Concordance With Hebrew and Greek Lexicon*, http://www.eliyah.com/lexicon.html.

Word definitions also from *Webster's New Collegiate Dictionary*, Springfield, MA: G. & C. Merriam Co., 1973.

Author's Note: Names have been changed to protect identities.

Previously published ISBN 0-9776871-0-4.

Cover design by Terry Clifton

Copyright © 2007 by Lorretta Kelley
All rights reserved

Library of Congress Control Number: 2007929197
International Standard Book Number: 978-1-59979-184-5

First Edition

07 08 09 10 11 — 987654321
Printed in the United States of America

This book is dedicated to my husband, Marcus J. Kelley, Sr.—my inspiration and road to freedom; to Isaiah Jones, Jr.; David and Doris Jones; Carolyn Kelley, Marcus, Jr., and Miriam Kelley—family members whose freedom and liberty in the faith have been a true inspiration to me continually; and to Christians everywhere in pursuit of answers and balance.

ACKNOWLEDGMENTS

THIS BOOK WOULD not be possible without the inspiration of the Holy Spirit and His patient endurance—to God be the glory.

A great deal of gratitude is offered to friends who have continually spoken words of encouragement. Several years have come and gone since the inception of this endeavor. During the wait, many friends have remained faithful and very supportive. Thank you. Your anticipation has been a source of strength.

A special thanks to all proofreaders, Bobbie Woodrome, Jennifer Mitchell, Shirley Palmer, and Marcus Kelley. Your comments and labor have been invaluable. Thank you for your honesty and for your love.

CONTENTS

PREFACE

AN ESTIMATED 5 to 7 million Americans have been involved in cults, or cult-like groups. Approximately 180,000 new cult recruits emerge yearly.[1] Legalism is cult-like in operation. This book takes a scriptural, straightforward look into the legalism lurking among us. The Bible warns us, both Old and New Testament, to beware of false teachers and false prophets who desire to enslave God's people. Their popularity indicates that Christians still enthusiastically embrace them.

Feel the passion of four people as they take us on their personal journey through bondage within the walls of legalism. See the warning signals they failed to heed. Note the carefully uncovered debilitating techniques employed by self serving, legalistic, and controlling people using Christianity as a pawn for merchandise. Sense the fear, shame, power and control, brainwashing, mind control, confusion, and much more that dominated their lives because they were in the wrong place of worship. Find out why one of them escapes with less injury than the others. Read how soul ties and fantasy bonding can entrap God's people and how difficult it is for them to leave their abusive environment.

We are called to an abundant life in Christ, not by our own works of righteousness (Titus 3:5). Otherwise, Christ died in vain. Those who taste real freedom and liberty in Christ will never want to go back to bondage again. Healing and restoration awaits the abused, the battered, and the confused. God really does care! There is a balm in Gilead (Jer. 8:22).

INTRODUCTION

THIS WORK IS inspired by a passion to see true Christians all over the world enjoying the abundant life which Christ said He came to deliver (John 10:10). The Good Shepherd gave His life for the sheep (John 10:11). Ought not the under shepherds also give their lives in service to protect and guard the sheep? Jesus said He was the door, and all who came in through Him would be saved. Through Him they would come and go and find pasture (food and needful supplies for true life) (John 10:9). The quality of life Jesus offers is what we desire to see in His church today.

Unusual levels of bondage and legalism are prevalent in some local assemblies, attempting to deplete believers of all that is theirs as heirs of God and joint-heirs with Christ, and conversely displaying the characteristics of a thief: to kill, steal, and destroy (John 10:10). This brings confusion about true Christianity, drawing some followers of Christ away from the church discouraged, declaring they shall never return. Their families and friends have also been afflicted, leaving them emotionally bruised and wounded.

Although some Christian organizations are clearly identified as legalistic by their practices, there are those who attend their assembly and enjoy the fellowship they encounter there. Someone put it this way, "One man's cult can be another man's utopia." However, for the thousands crying out for help, perhaps you can find solace in the Word of God as the pages of this reading lead you through some significant truths.

The Scriptures plainly tell us that "My people are destroyed for lack of knowledge" (Hosea 4:6). It goes on to implicate the religious leaders as guilty of keeping the people from knowing God. They were supposed to be spiritual leaders, but they became leaders in sin and disobedience.

Good leaders will produce good followers, making disciples who will reproduce and make other leaders in the kingdom of God. It is a joy to follow a man or woman of God as they lead in integrity, seeking to do the will of the Lord above their own will. God will draw others to follow their leadership to accomplish His will for the church.

There are important insights discussed in this book that will simplify the Scriptures and offer ultimate freedom for those who are seriously looking for answers and balance. The names of individuals and organizations are pseudonyms. This protects the privacy and the dignity of those who have moved on to victory in their lives.

This is a serious subject requiring much prayer—a long clear look at where the church, the body of Christ, is and a boldness to admit it. Over the eleven years I labored, I sought the Lord to deliver this writing as a work of love.

This book is not intended to bash, belittle, or bemoan any particular church, denomination, organization, or group. It is not intended to bring about rebellion or disrespect for the Christian calling or office of leadership as appointed by the Holy Spirit. It is intended to offer insight to anyone sincerely seeking enlightenment from the Word concerning a proper balance in the pulpit and church pews. For those who may have had problems in the church and are still struggling with their feelings and emotions, this book is intended to be part of the healing process that Christ offers as we turn to Him.

There is a balm in Gilead (Jer. 8:22).

PART I

IDENTIFYING THE BONDAGE

A SCRIPTURAL FOUNDATION

CHAPTER 1

REAL PEOPLE, REAL BONDAGE

I WOULD LIKE TO introduce four Christians whose lives changed drastically as a result of their involvement in a local, legalistic church fellowship. What happened in their lives caused them to question God, their spiritual leaders, and even their entire Christian lifestyle. Life as they once knew it would never be the same again.

Although it may be an unpopular thing to do, believers should question their spiritual environment and surroundings. Some teach that questioning is unlawful. However, it is not only proper to question your involvement, but it can be unwise not to do so. Many have been led astray because they failed to take notice and heed warning signals before they committed themselves spirit, soul, and body.

> Dear friends, do not believe everyone who claims to speak by the Spirit. You must test them to see if the spirit they have comes from God. For there are many false prophets in the world.
>
> —1 JOHN 4:1, NLT

In this fourth chapter the apostle John sets forth a warning. He tells believers that the Spirit of God dwells in them and leads them.

He wants us to know that false prophets make that same claim, that they too are indwelt and led by the Spirit of God. It is necessary, therefore, for believers to have enough information to accurately discern the difference between that which is holy and that which is profane; between that which is truly from the Spirit of God and that which is human in origin, fleshly, and evil.

One thing he warned believers to watch for was any teaching that contradicted what the apostles had already taught (2 John 8–10). John used a Greek word *dokimazo* to describe what believers should do. This word means "to test, to examine, to prove, to scrutinize, to see whether a thing is genuine or not." (See 1 John 4:1). He wanted us to check out these false prophets by a standard that never changes—the safe, uncompromising, unadulterated Word of our Living God. Not everyone will do this, to their own detriment.

Four Real People

To protect the dignity and privacy of these people, we have changed their names. Any similarities to others are purely coincidental. Legalism is a spirit, a spirit that maneuvers and operates the same everywhere, but perhaps in different degrees.

Susan

First we have forty-seven-year-old Susan Summerstone. She was miserable and unhappy at her local church fellowship. Physically and mentally worn, she admitted that she was experiencing very little peace. Perplexing thoughts overwhelmed her and many questions surfaced about her church membership. Although she prayed, she felt things were getting worse instead of better. What was she to do?

Susan quit attending her local church, thinking that would remove the pain quickly. This seemed to be her quickest and best recourse to alleviate the misery. She did not quit God, she just stopped attending the local fellowship. Susan was no stranger to Christianity or church. She loved the Lord and continued to seek Him for direction in her spiritual life.

How strange to be miserable serving God in your local church. Although many people blame the church, sometimes the struggle is within the individual, not in the church. The Psalmist wrote that we should "serve the Lord with gladness" (Ps. 100:1). Susan tried to do this, but was having difficulty at that particular church.

Susan examined her own motives and attitudes. Was it her home life, her husband, her children? She was puzzled and didn't understand what was troubling her. She still felt uncomfortable and empty inside, so she began fasting and praying for the Lord to reveal the source of her inner struggles. Often people blame someone else when they are unhappy. Susan's relationship with the Lord did not allow her to do that.

In her quest to find answers, the Lord taught her a number of key things. He revealed some inner wounds and hurts that were there since childhood. These were now causing problems in her devotion, fellowship, and worship.

Susan's time with the Lord opened a whole new world of understanding. Her past was influencing her future. It was affecting her decision-making ability, her esteem, and her view of life and other people. An attitude change was necessary. As the Lord began to put the pieces together, she began to understand why she was so miserable. Now the question was: when, where, and how was she going to feel whole again?

The local fellowship where Susan had attended was not equipped to handle her complex problems or offer any solutions. Instead of aiding her, the church had demanded perfection from her. When she did not live up to the leaders' expectations, manipulation, control, and guilt were launched against her. For more of Susan's perplexing thoughts, the questions that ran rampant in her mind, and her intriguing story read chapter 10, Warning Signal No. 2: Power and Control.

Barbara

Next meet Barbara Springfield, a leader in her church. She served with joy for a number of years. However, after ten years she began to notice that the joy she had once experienced was being replaced by a spirit of unrest.

Barbara kept silent about her feelings, her thoughts buried deep inside. She talked only to God, pondering in her heart what her internal disturbance might mean. In the months and years that followed, the unrest grew to a feeling of despair. Barbara was no longer happy attending this fellowship.

She perceived a distinctive shift in the vision and purpose of the fellowship. This was all right; she was not opposed to change. But some of the changes were obviously good, while others appeared to be unscriptural. She needed to talk to someone, but whom? She could talk to the Lord, and she did.

Barbara had entered the realm of religious error, but did not know it. Her own private world and the world of her family and friends were soon to be greatly affected. Read more details about Barbara's story in chapter 11, Warning Signal No. 3: Propagating the Spirit of Fear.

Robert

At first it was an emptiness that burdened Robert Winters. He found himself crying out to the Lord every day, wondering about the thoughts going through his mind. Sometimes he felt he understood. It was him; he just wasn't fitting in too well. At other times he was confused about church doctrine at the Tabernacle. Why was he so slow to get it? "What's wrong with me," he thought? "I know that it's good teaching. Everybody else seems to be very happy, so content." Sometimes thinking out loud he would say, "When will I just get with the program?"

Soon Robert began to feel fearful. He started feeling guilty about simple Christian living. There seemed to be a struggle, a war going on in his mind. At times he felt his manhood was challenged by the other members at the Tabernacle. There was also a problem with his authority at home. Where was this breakdown coming from? His family looked to him for stability, for security. Yet he felt his attitude, his commitment, and even his conversation were on shaky ground. Where was he to go with his questions, with his doubts?

Robert's wife and children did not have the same concerns that he had. In fact when he tried to discuss the situation, the problem seemed to reflect back to him. A breach in communication concerning the Tabernacle erupted in his family and threatened to bring major disharmony. Robert valued his family's love and respect, so he needed to do something quick. His responsibility was to protect and to provide for his family, and he knew that God often speaks to the head of the household when danger is threatening. Robert's wife believed that her husband's concerns were all in his mind. Were they? This man who loved God so much, and served Him faithfully for years, was now broken down on the inside and feeling like a complete failure. Read more about Robert's quest for internal peace in chapter 12, Warning Signal No. 4: The Transference of Guilt.

Curtis

Finally we have Curtis Fallbrook. Curtis was a believer who joined the Mission Church because he wanted to learn, to grow, and to do something significant for the Lord. Invited by a friend, he was excited to be there. The fellowship was the talk of the town. It had a reputation of being a thriving, biblically-based congregation with anointed, Bible-teaching leaders.

Everyone in Curtis' circle of friends had visited, and most were now joining. "This must be the place for me, too," Curtis thought.

Shortly after joining, Curtis confided in the Mission's pastor that he believed God was calling him to preach the gospel. He wanted to study and do whatever was necessary to fulfill that call. The pastor told Curtis to get involved in the church before preparing for his future in ministry.

However Curtis never felt really comfortable at the Mission Church. He tried hard to fit in and to be a part. His friends were delighted to be there and felt they had found the place where they could blossom and grow.

Even with all the excitement, Curtis felt strange about being there. Although he was involved, attended regularly, and participated in all the activities, he felt out of place. He was a praying man, so he soon realized that he was kicking against that which had come to caution him. After one year he left the Mission Church.

After seeking, Curtis found another church that he felt offered him more liberty and a better opportunity to pursue God's calling in his life. He was perplexed, however, about what had happened at the Mission Church. Curtis desperately wanted to be with his friends. Why had it worked for his friends and not for him? Why were they comfortable and fit in so well, but he didn't? Was there something wrong with him? These are a few of the questions that he meditated on as he moved forward and found another place to worship. Read more about Curtis' story and what he learned about trying to fit in. His story continues in chapter 9, Warning Signal No. 1: The Spirit of Elitism.

What's Wrong With Them?

It would be easy for a person on the outside to conclude that these four individuals had their own problems, which they blamed on the church they were attending. Of course they did have problems; we all have problems or concerns. Most Christians will admit that they have not reached the spirituality they're striving for. The apostle Paul tells us that even he was not yet perfected, but that he was pressing toward the mark for the prize of the high calling of God in Christ Jesus (Phil. 3:12, 14).

People leave churches all the time. In fact this generation of churchgoers seems to go from place to place for one reason or another. Are they really looking for Jesus, or are they seeking entertainment?

Not everyone can fit in just anywhere, most will agree to that. Each person should listen to the Holy Spirit and go where He leads. They should blossom where He plants them. Unfortunately not many people know or recognize the voice of the Holy Spirit, even though He is ever present with believers to lead and guide them into all truth.

Many Christian counselors attest that Susan, Barbara, Robert, and Curtis are just a small representation of the many Christians who love God and have dedicated their lives to the service of Christ. Although they are sincere servants, they end up in a local church or fellowship that is the wrong place for them. In their quest to grow they have been overtaken or overwhelmed by the spirit of legalism.

Appreciation must be mentioned for the great job that honorable and competent pastors are doing, as they fulfill God's call in their lives and the vision that God has given them to lead His people. It is often very hard to lead God's sheep. Pastors take a licking from some cruel, heartless believers. Many pastors have had to adjust their techniques to deal with people who are actually goats that have come in among the sheep. That's why it's important for pastors, as well as lay people, to be led by the Spirit of God when they step into the office of leadership.

On the other hand, it is sad to see what has happened to some of God's precious people. Some of those who really are His sheep have greatly suffered at the hands of manipulating, controlling, and dogmatic leaders who drive, rather than lead, the flock of God.

Susan, Barbara, Robert, and Curtis's experiences are intertwined throughout the pages of this book. They have run head-on into the paths of legalists who snatched their peace and like a demolition crew devastated the lives of unsuspecting Christians.

There is a great need for balance in the pulpit and pews! The entire Word of God is written so that believers can be free from the bondage of sin and Satan. It is written so that we can be free to live an abundant, wholesome, and productive life in Christ Jesus. We should not be in bondage to one another.

I believe the words of Jesus ring true and give us a simple key. "If ye continue in my word, then are ye my disciples indeed; And ye shall know the truth, and the truth shall make you free" (John 8:31–32).

It is not my intention to bash the great leaders, pastors, bishops, and elders that are serving God today in integrity and truth. It is intended, however, to uncover some of the strategies used by the ungodly to ensnare innocent Christians, and to identify how these same Christians are easily caught in abusive situations. This writing will expose some of the wiles of the evil one, our adversary, as he manipulates the minds and motives of self-seeking, self-appointed leaders.

There is hope for you and your loved ones, for anyone currently trapped by the deceit of cunning leaders, possibly even a leader from any organization, religious or otherwise. This is a message of hope.

You may have been wooed into their confidence. They may have subtly snatched your dignity, manipulated your mind, separated you from your friends and family, and merchandised your gifts and talents. There is hope. You can be healed and restored.

The ultimate plan of false leaders is to brainwash you into believing a lie. They are capable of raping your personhood, your soul, and sometimes even your body. Do not be fooled by their sneaky tricks. They are devious and underhanded.

Many lives have been severely disrupted, but there are those who fail to face the reality of these things. We see it on television, but cannot fathom it in our own fellowship. That's too close. It happens to someone else's family, but not in our family; in another city, but not in our city.

The answer to any dilemma has always been Jesus. If we lack wisdom, we are invited to ask of Him. He must be the focus and center of our entire Christian life. If we have questions or if life perplexes us, we must go back to the one who created life, God. Examine His truths about life and living, men and women.

I sincerely pray that as you continue to read this book it will be a true source of illumination and enlightenment that will set you absolutely free in Him, Christ Jesus, who loves you and gave His life for you.

Christ is the truth, the way and the life. (See John 14:6.) He is our source of truth, the perfect standard of what is right. Look to Him now, my friend, and be blessed!

CHAPTER 2

BONDAGE AND BALANCE DEFINED

LET'S LOOK A little closer at two words we shall consistently use in this book: bondage and balance. First, from the many definitions listed in *Webster's Dictionary*, the following definitions were carefully selected and adequately describe the words *bondage* and *balance*. Secondly we must also look at the biblical definitions of these two words so that we are careful to use them in the proper context. Please take special note of each definition listed. This is not an English lesson, but it is important.

Bondage

> 1) a state of being bound, usually by compulsion (as of law or mastery); 2) captivity {the bondage of the Israelites in Egypt} 3) servitude or subjugation to a controlling person or force.

The synonym (a word that means the same) for bondage is *servitude*. This word is found among the words used to define bondage. When we look at the meaning of servitude we will find additional understanding.

Servitude

> 1) a condition in which one lacks liberty, especially to determine one's course of action or way of life.

This is a straightforward statement. Let me again restate the meaning of servitude: it is a condition in which a person has no liberty—freedom—to determine his own course of action or way of life.

Now the Bible dictionary comes right out and calls bondage, slavery. In Galatians, Paul admonishes the Galatia church: "Stand fast therefore in the liberty wherewith Christ hath made us free, and be not entangled again with the yoke of bondage" (Gal. 5:1). The Greek word translated *bondage* is *douleia*. The English translation is slavery, which means "to be in bondage."

The strength of the message conveyed by Paul in Galatians 5:1 is clearly recognized. The Amplified Bible illuminates the same verse this way: "In [this] freedom Christ has made us free [and completely liberated us]; stand fast then, and do not be hampered and held ensnared and submit again to a yoke of slavery [which you have once put off]."

Paul is reminding us that Christ lived, died, was buried, and rose again from the dead to set us free from a long list of laws and regulations that we could never keep. Through this freedom we can now serve God unselfishly and willingly without trying to keep these rules. The legalists were trying to yoke the Galatians with Judaism. A yoke is a symbol of slavery.

Bondage is demonstrated in a great number of Christian churches and other organizations, just as it was when Paul preached to the Galatian Christians. God, our Heavenly Father, is not the author of this activity. Let's call it what it is: *bondage in the pulpit and pews.*

Balance

> 1) a means of judging or deciding; (a pair of scales); 2) a stability produced by even distribution of weight on each side of the vertical axis; 3) the ability to retain one's balance, mental or emotional steadiness.

The following words are synonyms for balance: composure, equanimity, poise, self-possession.

Equanimity is evenness of mind, especially under stress. It is having composure or the right disposition. It is a characteristic of one who is self-possessed and not easily disturbed or perturbed. In the context of this reading material, we certainly are not suggesting that there will never be times when Christians are "*easily disturbed or perturbed.*" That would be an unbalanced statement. Many of life's events can, and will cause us to be disturbed. A person who has evenness of mind and exercises balance is not a person who is unaffected by the reality of what is happening, or a person without any flaws.

However, when in the company of his leaders and peers, a person who exercises balance will:

1. have the ability to make *sensible decisions* as to what he believes and how he lives;

2. have a normal *stability* in his mind and will;

3. demonstrate *mental and emotional steadiness*;

4. have *confidence* not in himself, but *in Christ Jesus.* He, being wholly submitted to the lordship of Christ, and not to the lordship of man or of himself;

5. *will walk in a calmness and a freedom* from labor, responsibility, or strain as it relates to his relationship with God and his Christian walk of faith.

Balance is composure. It is *rest*.

Most Christians have not yet reached the place of rest that Christ offers each of us who will come to Him. (See Matthew 11:28.) As we grow, we move toward basking in this rest, and our leaders should be pointing in that direction—toward Christ, the rest-giver.

It stands to reason that the antonym (a word of opposite meaning) for balance, or composure, is discomposure.

So it is important for Christians to understand the difference between *balance* and *bondage*. If you are

1. significantly discomposed;

2. disturbed in your spirit;

3. losing the capacity for collected thought or decisive action because you are enslaved to a set of rules or to someone in authority, then take time to consider the fact that you may be in bondage—the difference should be clear.

As God's beloved you should pray and seek His guidance for understanding and for freedom from the discomforting realm of bondage!

CHAPTER 3

HEAVEN'S WEIGHTS AND MEASURES

For the Lord seeth not as man seeth; for man looketh on the outward appearance, but the Lord looketh on the heart.

—1 SAMUEL 16:7

IN 1 SAMUEL 8:4 we find the prophet Samuel conversing with the elders of Israel. It seems the elders were no longer content having the Lord God of heaven to reign over them; they wanted a visible king like the other nations around them. Samuel prayed to the Lord who instructed him to warn the people about the results of having a king. The people persisted in their request, and the Lord granted their wish.

Saul, son of Kish, was chosen and anointed by the Lord as the first king of Israel. Although he was tall, handsome, brave, patriotic, and had a zeal for the people, he was not chosen because of his outward appearance. Saul possessed other qualities such as humility and self-control. He started his rule over Israel as a loyal, committed king. Unfortunately he did not remain that way. He was plagued by a spirit of pride, egotism, and jealousy. The continual abuse of his power and his rebellion ultimately led to his decline and downfall.

God rejected Saul and repented that He had made him king. Saul's life stands as an example to leaders today that you can be chosen by God to lead His people, but you must remain obedient, submissive, and yielded to His authority to continue in His favor. Following God's rejection of Saul as king, He sent Samuel to the house of Jesse the Bethlehemite to choose a king for himself among Jesse's eight sons. Now the first son, Eliab, stood before the man of God and Samuel, who was looking at him as though he was surely the one the Lord wanted to anoint as king, but the Lord refused Eliab.

God told Samuel that it was he, (man) who looked on the outward appearance—countenance, height, stature. Man looks to see if someone is short or tall, fat or skinny, blonde or brunette, blue or brown eyes, fair or dark complexion, and all the other characteristics by which man measures for his own acceptance or rejection. Outward characteristics should never be used to measure a man for a leadership role.

As the One who sees spiritually, God knows the intent and character of the heart. Men should seek God for His wisdom in choosing a spiritual leader.

Followers of Christ are to be known by their love. They should manifest the fruit of the spirit: love, joy, peace, longsuffering, gentleness, goodness, faith, meekness, and temperance (Gal. 5:22).

Christ said in His sermon on the mount, "Blessed are the pure in heart, for they shall see God" (Matt. 5:8). That purity was a call for sincerity and honesty in all of His followers, not just for those who were called to be leaders among them.

In 2 Peter 1:5–7 Peter stated that believers should make an effort to improve their faith by adding virtue, knowledge, self-control, patience, godliness, brotherly kindness, and love. These eight characteristics, when diligently applied, will produce a continuous growth pattern in your life and render your Christian service meaningful and useful. Consider the following results of these eight characteristics.

1. Faith will help you to grow spiritually; it is the Christian's foundation.

2. Virtue will produce moral excellence, strong character, and discipline.

3. Knowledge will help believers to understand what God thinks and values, as opposed to their own opinions.

4. Self-control will demonstrate an ability to lead oneself as well as the ability to lead others.

5. Patience will produce endurance and enable believers to consistently do what is right.

6. Godliness will help believers to live a lifestyle that honors God.

7. Brotherly kindness will demonstrate the love of Christ in all relationships.

8. *Love* will identify the characteristic of God within us.

If we profess Christianity we are to be governed by its laws, principles, and precepts. The difference between Christians and non-Christians should be the distinctive change the Holy Spirit makes on the inside as they yield to His sanctification. Christians cannot change by themselves, because they were born sinners. But if anyone is in Christ, they are a new creation (2 Cor. 5:17)!

I'm reminded of an old hymn by Rufus H. McDaniel and Charles H. Gabriel that speaks of the wonderful change that occurs when Christ enters the yielded vessel.

Since Jesus Came Into My Heart

What a wonderful change in my life has been wrought,
  since Jesus came into my heart!

I have light in my soul for which long I had sought,
  since Jesus came into my heart.

I have ceased from my wand'ring and going astray,
  since Jesus came into my heart.

And my sins, which were many, are all washed away,
  since Jesus came into my heart.

Chorus:

Since Jesus came into my heart,

Since Jesus came into my heart,

Floods of joy o'er my soul like the sea billows roll,
  since Jesus came into my heart![1]

What leader would want to infiltrate the life of a believer, or dare to damage or compete with the wonderful work Christ has begun in his heart! Christianity is a call to integrity, soundness, and wholeness; and an adherence to a standard and code of values. Outside of Christianity, no one is able to consistently walk in this level of integrity. Legalism is designed to keep a person trying to be right and righteous in their own strength.

Even though every faculty of man was affected by the Fall in the Garden of Eden, within each man there is still the image of the Creator, a spirit which gives to man the standard for right and godliness as opposed to wrong and ungodliness. This candle or lamp is man's moral measure, it is a means of self-examination given by God. (See John 8:9 and Proverbs 20:27.)

A man's character is of great importance, for it tells the worth of a man from the inside, as measured by God. Character is what we are. Reputation is what people think we are.

Heaven's Eyes

The eyes of heaven are always upon us. Although we may think that God cannot see us, He does. He is in heaven beholding the good and the evil. The Bible also tells us: "For the eyes of the Lord run to and fro throughout the whole earth, to show himself strong in the behalf of them whose heart is perfect toward him" (2 Chron. 16:9). This is what the seer, Hanani, said to Asa, the king of Judah. When Asa relied on the Lord and followed His instructions in battle, he always had victory. In this instance the king had hooked up and conspired with men to aid him in his battles and God was greatly displeased. The consequences of trusting man rather than God in times of need were always very disappointing.

Job, God's Servant, Asks for His Integrity to Be Weighed

The Book of Job offers a great deal of understanding to the suffering of the righteous, trusting God during difficult times, and the inward and outward struggles of dealing with the opinions of men. Many people are determined to tell others what they think of them, good and bad things, so most Christians have had to deal with this issue. Hurtful words often leave a lasting imprint on a person's life.

Sometimes what others say about us weighs heavier than what God says about us. Although some things are true, they are better not said, especially when they damage someone internally. Some people seem to carry around a measuring stick to measure the good and bad in everyone they meet. I would rather my life and character be measured by a just standard, which can only be from a standard set by God in heaven.

> Let me be weighed in an even balance, that God may know mine integrity.
>
> —JOB 31:6

God confirmed the character of Job in chapter 1, verse 8 by announcing to Satan that there was none like Job in the earth, a perfect and an upright man, one that reverenced God, and escheweth (avoided) evil. However, as we read further in the book, multiple disasters left Job's life and character questionable in the eyes of his friends. He lost his children, his cattle, and most of his possessions. In addition, Job became very sick in his body. The situation looked pretty bad from where his friends were standing. They were convinced that he must be a sinner.

In Job chapters 6 and 7, Job makes his objection and defends his own integrity in response to his friend's, Eliphaz's claim in chapter 5 that he is being chastened by God because he has sinned. This defense is his attempt to clear himself of the crimes of which his friend had falsely accused him. Job had a strong internal conviction that he was a man of character.

He was secure in that about himself. Wouldn't you like to have that same kind of security about yourself? It is possible if you believe heaven's report about you rather than the devil's.

Isn't it just like the devil to call you one thing, while God has called you something totally different! God saw Job as an upright man; the devil, speaking through Job's friends, saw him as a sinner.

That should give us all something to think about. We should not concentrate on what others say or think about us, but only what the Word of God has already declared about us as born again believers. Of course, God can use others to help us grow spiritually by pointing out things that need to change in our lives. All things should be said and done in love.

In spite of his present circumstances and in defense of his sincerity, Job uses chapter 31 to address his friends and acquit himself of specific accusations including: wantonness, uncleanness, adultery, haughtiness, fraud, injustice in business, etc. Verse 6 particularly addresses his innocence as it relates to dishonesty. Notice that he is willing to be weighed by a just (right) *balance* (scales), so that it can be confirmed that nothing was obtained by vanity. He is willing to give up the entire cargo if there is found any prohibited goods or anything that was not gained honestly.

He states, as we read further:

> If my step has turned out of [God's] way, and my heart has gone the way my eyes [covetously] invited, and if any spot has stained my hands with guilt, then let me sow and let another eat; yes, let the produce of my field or my offspring be rooted out.
>
> —JOB 31:7–8, AMP

Would to God that all who are called to be leaders walked in such integrity! Be inspired, dear reader, to bring your heart back to understanding the real importance of serving God and man with integrity and purity of heart.

Belshazzar, King of Babylon

> And this is the writing that was written, MENE, MENE, TEKEL, UPHARSIN.
>
> —DANIEL 5:25

Can you remember reading about King Belshazzar, king of Babylon (Dan. 5:23), who defiled the holy vessels of the temple in the city of Jerusalem by drinking wine out of them while praising his gods of gold, silver, brass, iron, wood, and stone? While he was drinking, carousing, and having a jolly good time, the fingers of a man's hand appeared to write on the wall of his palace. All that the king could see was part of the hand that wrote. This brought him great fear!

He called for the astrologers, the Chaldeans (diviners), and the soothsayers (enchanters) to interpret this writing. None of them could interpret it. Belshazzar was gripped with an immense fear!

The queen saved the day when she recommended Daniel, whom she described as "a man in your kingdom," in whom is the Spirit of the Holy God, who had

1. light and understanding;

2. wisdom like the wisdom of the gods;

3. an excellent spirit;

4. knowledge and understanding;

5. the gift of interpreting dreams and showing hard sentences;

6. and dissolving of doubts.

She told Belshazzar to let Daniel be called and he would show the interpretation (Dan. 5:11–12).

It is very interesting to note the queen's comments about Daniel. Although she was not listed as a godly woman, but rather a heathen, let me repeat a summary of what she thought of this man Daniel: he had a preeminent (extraordinary) and excellent spirit, and was mightily used of God in knowledge and great understanding.

What are unbelievers saying about Christian leaders today? What are they recognizing in their lives? Honesty, integrity, uprightness, righteousness? Can they see an excellent spirit? Can they say that they are mightily used of God in knowledge and great understanding? Thank God, He is certainly using a great number of Christian leaders who proclaim the truth and walk upright before Him. The body of Christ is blessed because of their ministry in the world.

As leaders are being used today, so Daniel was indeed a man of God who was chosen for that particular day and time and for that specific incident to glorify God. Daniel was also around when Belshazzar's grandfather, Nebuchadnezzar, erred. Now an old man, he stands before yet another king to proclaim the justice of God. He gives the following understanding to the writing on the wall:

> This is the interpretation of the thing: MENE; God hath numbered thy kingdom, and finished it. TEKEL; Thou art weighed in the balances, and art found wanting. PERES [UPHARSIN in Aramaic]; thy kingdom is divided, and given to the Medes and Persians.
>
> —DANIEL 5:26–28

The king and his actions had been weighed by the divine, just *balances* of Almighty God, who knew his true character. God knows all of us.

The New Testament tells us that Jesus also knew the thoughts of men before they were verbalized. (See Matt. 9:4 and Luke 5:22, 6:8, 9:47.)

Daniel reveals God's thoughts about Belshazzar. But notice that judgment was not given until the facts had been first evaluated for worth and significance. That's what "weighed in the balance" means. The biblical definition of the word balance is:

> To ponder; to give good heed. To consider carefully and at length.

God did not make a hasty decision, instead He mused over it, contemplated, and meditated on it. King Belshazzar had been found "wanting" by the scales of divine justice. He was found unworthy, vain, and light; an empty man of no weight or consideration; seriously defective and of poor quality. This was according to God's standard of measurement, not man's. This was heaven's measurement.

Belshazzar's kingdom was tested and numbered. His character was flawed. He did wrong and caused his followers to do wrong as well. Should you attempt to feel sorry for him, or think that your character can't be as bad as his because you did not do what he did, read further in Daniel 5, verses 18 through 23. In these scriptures Daniel reminds Belshazzar of his grandfather Nebuchadnezzar's rise to glory and honor, and his fall because of *pride*. The details are startling. Pride is one of the key issues in the downfall of many leaders. See chapter 9 where we discuss further the spirit of elitism.

Daniel also warns Belshazzar that he too was lifted up with *pride* just like his grandfather. His desecration of the Lord's holy vessels was a deliberate act of defiance toward the living God. He drank from the Lord's sacred vessels to honor the pagan gods of Babylon. This was blatant dishonor of the one true God. Belshazzar had full knowledge of the tragedy that had befallen his grandfather Nebuchadnezzar for the sin of pride and rebellion. There was no excuse for Belshazzar. That night he was killed.

Can Christian leaders today be weighed by divine, just balances and be found worthy, rather than wanting like Belshazzar? As we look at our own lives today, are we believers who fear God and escheweth evil, like God's servant Job?

There are many examples in Scripture, and also in our world today. If you are one who walks in pride demonstrating a haughty spirit, you pay a high price. That price is a fall and destruction. When we lose the favor of God, we have lost everything.

God looks at the heart of His servants; what was observed about Belshazzar's heart? The scripture confirms that his heart

1. allowed him to desecrate the holy vessels of God, which were used in the temple for God's purpose;

2. allowed him to praise false gods;

3. did not glorify the God of heaven in whose hands his breath was;

4. became full of fear when he saw the handwriting.

He was a leader who lost favor with God, because his heart was not right. God found him wanting (deficient).

God is glorified by our obedience. We honor Him by respecting the position or office of leadership to which He has appointed us. We honor God by remaining humble. We cannot afford for one minute to think that what is accomplished in our churches, ministries, and organizations is done by the might of our own hands.

Although Nebuchadnezzar was a heathen king, Daniel reminded his grandson Belshazzar that the kingdom in which his grandfather reigned was given unto him by Almighty God—the one true God. It was He who gave Nebuchadnezzar glory, majesty, and honor. But he who was lifted up in pride fell very low at the hands of an all-seeing, all-knowing, all-powerful God. Pride is truly an ugly spirit and originates from the devil. Guard yourselves from its clutches, because it seeks to dominate every one of God's children.

Someone might be tempted to say, "But that was Old Testament, we're living under grace now in the New Testament." My friends, God's grace is seen from Genesis to Revelation. Take a good look. He has always been a faithful God of grace and love.

Leaders should never present themselves as deity, or in any way insinuate that the flock of God must bow down and worship at their feet. It is not likely that a man can control the personal lives of all those who are under his leadership, as well as his own personal life and destiny. That attitude is dangerous. Instead leaders should let God be God. He's doing a fantastic job of being Himself, ruler of the universe, Lord of all.

Hallelujah!

Some lessons in life are learned through trial and error and experience. Other lessons though are learned through reading the Scriptures and gleaning the wisdom from its pages. We are not always afforded a trial and error period where we can say, "Oops, I missed it!" There will be consequences for all of our choices and actions. Sometimes the consequences are not as severe. Thank God for that! Sometimes we're just covered by the blood of Jesus and His mercy spares us.

We must learn from the Word of God so that our consequences are not as devastating as the examples already set before us. It becomes a matter of do or die in some situations. Obey or your ministry perishes. Walk in the Word or you lose your family and all you have. How many ministries have we witnessed in the last thirty years that have perished before our very eyes: too many.

Let's pause now and pray this prayer together:

> *Lord help me to learn humility and not to follow a path of destruction. Inspire me to seek Your face continually; give me an obedient, submissive spirit, so that I can flow in the understanding and wisdom of God. Help me to understand that the fear of the Lord is the beginning of wisdom, and that as one of Your leaders I am an under shepherd of Christ, the Chief Shepherd. I desire to walk as a balanced believer. I desire to demonstrate Your love to everyone, and to be a reflection of the loveliness of Christ. Amen.*

CHAPTER 4

THE FOUNTAIN OF LIFE

For with thee is the fountain of life: in thy light shall we see light.

—PSALM 36:9

PSALM 36 CONTRASTS the wickedness of man with the steadfastness of God. In verses 1 through 4 David graphically describes nine characteristics of the wicked:

1. His heart says there is no fear of God before his eyes.
2. He flatters himself in his own eyes.
3. His iniquity is found to be hateful.
4. The words of his mouth are iniquity and deceit.
5. He has left off being wise.
6. He has left off being good.
7. He devises mischief on his bed.
8. He sets himself in a way that is not good.
9. He does not abhor evil.

Beginning in verse 5, he exalts at least nine attributes of God.

1. Mercy
2. Faithfulness
3. Righteousness
4. Great judgment

5. Loving kindness
6. Goodness
7. Life
8. Light
9. Justice

In verse 9 David unveils a powerful truth. God is not only the source of our natural life, but our spiritual life as well. All energy and assistance in our sanctified souls, all authority, and all efficiencies (effective useful operations) are from Him. Our very happiness consists of the revelation, delight, and enjoyment of Him. God is both our life and light. Things are made clear for us as we walk in His light.

If we stop walking in that light, a difference is immediately noticed. That difference is internal. Your soul knows when something has gone awry. You can try to ignore it, or you can begin to seek God's face for answers. Should we choose to ignore God's warnings, we can become immune to His truths. We then leave ourselves vulnerable to Satan's attacks, ensnarement, and ultimate bondage. To this end we shall examine the lives of a few people who ignored the whispers of their souls.

The Available Fountain

One of my favorite Christian songs concerning salvation is an old hymn written by William Cowper. This song comes as an invitation and proclamation of what salvation has to offer anyone who will come to Jesus. No matter what state we're in when we come, we come as sinners needing a Savior.

It does not matter how vile a sinner we are, the shed blood of Jesus is able to wash all sin away—the sins of the thief, murderer, whoremonger, prostitute, derelict, winebibber, alcoholic, drug abuser, any abuser; molesters, gangsters, cult member, heathen, false religious, homosexuals, heterosexuals, any sinner, anybody.

Just come! His blood will wash all your sins away. He is able to keep you, and His blood will never lose its power to wash and continually cleanse you of all sin and unrighteousness. Just come!

It is important for us to understand and receive Christ's atonement for our sins, yesterday, today, and forever. Our life is in Christ and our salvation is not to be taken lightly. Christ gave His life that we might know the Father. Peter stated in Matthew 16:16 that Jesus was the "Christ, the Son of the living God." This truth came to him as a revelation from God our Father. We must all have this same revelation from God. It is upon this great truth and revelation that Jesus proclaimed "the gates of hell shall not prevail against it" (Matt. 16:18). In other words, Satan and all the evil in the world cannot destroy the church of Jesus Christ.

It is also recorded that William Cowper took the words of this old hymn from the Book of Zechariah, Chapter 13:1: "In the future there will be a fountain, where David's descendants and the people of Jerusalem can wash away their sin and guilt" (CEV). Once again we have an affirmation of the cleansing blood of Christ Jesus for all those who truly repent and are sorry for their sins.

The fountain of life. What a great beginning! A new life in Jesus. What joy, what peace, what love, what security!

There Is a Fountain Filled With Blood

There is a fountain filled with blood drawn
   from Immanuel's veins.

And sinners plunged beneath that flood lose
   all their guilty stains:

The dying thief rejoiced to see that fountain
   in his day.

And there may I, though vile as he, wash all
   my sins away.

Dear dying Lamb, thy precious blood shall
    never lose its pow'r,

Till all the ransomed Church of God be saved
    to sin no more:

E'er since by faith I saw the stream thy flowing
    wounds supply,

Redeeming love has been my theme and shall
    be till I die.[1]

The man who penned these words lived from 1731 to 1800. History tells of his father's desire for him to study and become a lawyer. Upon completion of his studies, William Cowper prepared to take the final exam when fear gripped him. He became desperately afraid of taking the bar exam, and had a mental breakdown. He even attempted suicide. William spent eighteen months in an insane asylum. It was during his confinement that he began studying the Bible. In 1764, at the age of thirty-three, William's relationship with Christ had developed and he understood as never before the forgiveness of sin.

A Happy Beginning

At the beginning of our Christian walk we're on top of the world and it seems like nothing can possibly go wrong with our great heritage in God. Think about it. Can you still remember how excited you were when you became a new Christian? For some it was the very first time you had been to church. For others it meant that you were no longer just routinely going to church, singing in the choir, serving as an usher, working in the nursery, or performing other religious duties. Like William Cowper's story, you realized that God is real. Our Heavenly Father had revealed Jesus Christ to you in your innermost being, and you were on fire for Him. You had now experienced the Fountain of Life, and things couldn't get better!

People who knew you saw that your life had really changed and some of them began asking, "Why?" Can you remember how eager and excited you were to share with everybody how Christ had come into your life and changed you from the inside out? Even though there were some who rejected you, it didn't matter; you were both confident and secure in your newfound relationship with Jesus. Your attitude changed. You went through behavior modifications. You became a brand-new creature, just like the Scripture said. Thus began your journey of discovering who Jesus really is.

With each morning you enjoyed a fresh sensation of facing the day with Christ. It was just good to be alive in Jesus. The church you were attending was everything you wanted it to be: good teaching and preaching, an outreach program, evangelistic programs, a missions program, a thriving youth ministry, prayer and fasting, and many other activities.

The church promised to be just what a New Testament church should be. It was exciting to go to the meetings, because God was moving by His Spirit and new things were happening. Enthusiasm was at an all-time high. It was a community of believers, a real family with everyone sharing the same hopes and dreams.

As a mother said to her young child, "Now what is wrong with this picture?"

Things Changed, Questions Arise

Time has passed and you notice that things have changed around the fellowship. A few years have come and gone. You feel you've grown spiritually, yet you begin to sense a change. Here are some questions that may come to mind as your spirit man alerts you that something may be awry.

1.   Is it me?

2.   What could be wrong?

3.   Who can I talk to? To whom can I turn for help?

4.   Can I share my crazy thoughts and concerns with my leaders?

5.   Will they resent me?

6.   Will the information I share get twisted and distorted? (I've observed this with others.)

7.   Are my motives and comments now in question?

8.   What happened to that fountain of life?

9.   Why are they staring at me?

10. Do they still trust me?

11. Will I be asked to leave the church?

12. Does God still love me?

If you are bombarded with thoughts and questions such as these, you might be in the beginning stages of a bondage environment. The Holy Spirit could be sending a warning signal to you. Although we do not advocate the sheep telling the shepherd what to do, accusing their leaders with impure motives, or having attitudes of disrespect, these kinds of questions entering your mind may be a cautionary sign that you might be entering an area dominated by fear.

To answer some of these questions, you must first examine the Word of God as it pertains to your own Christian discipleship and disciplined lifestyle. Then you can also see what the Bible has to say about the roles and responsibilities of Christian leadership. In the next chapter we'll take a look at what the Scriptures do say about God's appointed leaders.

CHAPTER 5

A BALANCED LOOK AT BIBLICAL QUALIFICATIONS FOR LEADERSHIP

THROUGHOUT THE BIBLE we read of God's call and appointment of men and women to lead. They were submissive servants. They were severely chastised and/or removed from leadership when they no longer obeyed the God who had called them. Some even lost their lives. As God's representatives, they were to manifest the loving godly authority that had been delegated to them. A good example of this delegation would be Moses, who exercised authority before Pharaoh with his rod.

They were to be godly leaders. Some were called seers, judges, prophets, priests, kings; others were called elders, bishops, pastors, deacons, apostles, evangelists, teachers, etc. But all functioned as servants, first to God, then to God's people.

When God instituted these offices and positions, He did so to fashion and mold a people for Himself. Leaders were to point the people toward God and toward His Christ.

Functioning under God's headship, leaders and followers were to walk in obedience and holiness. This would, in turn, yield success and prosperity for their lives, giving glory to God. God's people were to be as lights in the earth, so that others would know that there is a God in heaven and desire to have Him in their lives. What a plan! God's plan of redemption!

The Pastor and the Church

And I say also unto thee, That thou art Peter, and upon this rock I will build my church; and the gates of hell shall not prevail against it.

—MATTHEW 16:18

A pivotal conversation arose one day in the region of Caesarea Philippi when Jesus asked His disciples a question, "Whom do men say that I the Son of man am?" They discussed the people's comments about His identity. The Pharisees and other religious leaders had already made it plain what they thought about Jesus: He was not one of them (Matt. 16:13–20).

It was the second probing and leading question from the Savior, however, that was to reveal a great and powerful truth to His followers. Jesus asked, "But who do you say that I am?" (Matt. 16:15, NKJV). Peter then uttered a revelation straight from the throne of our Heavenly Father, "You are the Christ, The Son of the living God" (Matt. 16:16, NKJV). This is exactly what Christ wanted to hear. It is on the revelation of this truth that Christ promises He will build—establish—His church. This passage of Scripture is often believed to be the first mention of the New Testament church (Greek: *ekklesia*), the called-out ones.

Those who have accepted Jesus Christ as Lord and Savior are identified as His church. God gave His Son Jesus to be head of the church, and the church is to be subject to Him.

He wants to present a glorious church, not having spot, wrinkle, or any such thing, holy and without blemish (Eph. 5:27).

Christ walked the earth and taught His followers principles and precepts for growth and development. Although many would sin and miss the mark, God's redemptive plan was put into place before the foundation of the world. God is love (1 John 4:8).

Jesus is presented as our advocate (Greek: *parakletos*). An advocate is one who pleads with God the Father for the pardon of our sins. With His pleadings we have confidence that our sins are forgiven: past, present, and future.

Ephesians 4:11 also documents and outlines God's plan for the care and growth of His people. God gave gifts to the church. Today we call them the five-fold ministry gifts. They are people who are called by God to function in these capacities. They have been anointed and appointed. We have the apostle who governs; the prophet who guides; the evangelist who gathers; the pastor who guards, and the teacher who grounds.

What an awesome plan! Functioning as God has designed, each spiritual office perfects and fully equips His saints so that they might do the work of the ministry (Eph. 4:11–16).

Today, unfortunately, some of the qualifications, roles, and responsibilities of spiritual offices have been diluted and distorted. A few men and women of God have chosen position, titles, power, and money over the joy of following God's design and plan. The trade has cost the church (God's people) a pretty price.

Pastor literally means "shepherd, one who guards and feeds the flock of God." He is appointed as God's delegated authority, the under shepherd, while Jesus remains our Chief Shepherd. All believers need the tender, vigilant oversight of a diligent, loving Pastor.

God was very careful and specific in His call, qualifications, and requirements of pastors. His church is the apple of His eye, and only a qualified shepherd who is willing to be a servant first of all would suffice to oversee His beloved.

In 1 Timothy 3:1 the scripture tells us that if a man understands the call of God within him and desires to walk in this office, he desires a good work.

Then in chapter 3, verse 2, Timothy uses two key words, "must be" to describe a list of qualifications for the bishop (elders or pastors). Please notice that the scripture did not say should be, could be, or ought to be, it clearly says he "must be."

Can you see that our heavenly Father wants only those who are wholly His to shepherd His people.

A Brief Look at the Pastors' Responsibilities

As overseers, a great work of ministry is charged to pastors. They are to instruct us in righteousness, correct us, teach us the way, reprove, rebuke, and exhort us. This is all to be done in love and with a spirit of meekness.

Through the ministry of the pastors the church will grow spiritually and fulfill the purposes of God. One result is that Christians will not be easily deceived by the wiles (deceits and strategies) of the devil.

Since Pastors are charged by God to shepherd the Church, they are admonished to:

1.	Labor in word and doctrine	1 Timothy 5:17
2.	Rule over	Hebrews 13:17
3.	Perfect the saints	Ephesians 4:12
4.	Feed and take the oversight	1 Peter 5:2, Acts 20:28
5.	Preach the Word, reprove, rebuke, exhort	2 Timothy 4:2
6.	Pray for the sick	James 5:14

What great rewards are experienced on both sides when the right pastor is placed with the right people. The evidence of success is overwhelming. Thank God for all of His loving and dedicated pastors who are dutifully serving the flock. We love and appreciate every one of you!

First Peter 5:1–4 instructs pastors to

1. *feed* by preaching the unadulterated Word of God;

2. *take the oversight* by personal care and watchfulness;

3. be *examples to the flock* by practicing holiness, self-denial, and the other Christian attributes, which they preach and recommend to the people.[1]

Pastors must serve the people willingly. They must not be in it for personal or dishonest gain, or to have someone to lord over.

Contrary to God's plan, men and women have taken on the pastoral position as a lucrative career or as a position of power.

Prayerfully you will be able to discern the marked difference in the pastor who has been called and appointed by God, and one who has been committee-appointed. Of course it is possible for God to anoint a committee of people to pray and seek Him during their selection process. He is a God of order. But too often men and women have not been *sent* by God, they just *went* on their own. Some may be frustrated with failed attempts to function in existing organizations. Others may be rebellious and unwilling to submit. Whatever the reason, it is true that not all are from God—and this spells trouble.

The Plan

Pastors were never intended to be god *to* us, or be god *for* us. They are not qualified, nor should they ever attempt in any way to be god *over* us. The pastor is to guard and watch over the flock of God, for God, like a shepherd watches over his sheep. Unfortunately this is not a reality in many churches. Many pastors today are in need of a pastor themselves—a mentor with whom they can communicate spiritually, a father in the gospel who walks in integrity and has a visibly sound relationship with the Lord.

Christ taught His disciples an important truth recorded in Mark 10:35–45 and Matthew 20:20–28. James and John came to Him and requested that they be allowed to sit, one on His right hand and the other on His left hand, in His kingdom. His response to them was in the form of a question; He asked if they could drink from the cup of sorrow and be baptized with the baptism of affliction that He must endure. Not knowing the future, they both responded, "We are able." Jesus, knowing their future, assured them that they would suffer sorrow and affliction. However, He could not grant them their request for a position of honor, since it was reserved only for those for whom it was prepared and ordained.

Naturally the other ten disciples were disturbed because James and John made this request of Jesus. But Jesus used this opportunity to teach them a valuable lesson; if you want to be chief, you must serve everybody.

The desire to be great is a strong spirit in Christendom today. Greatness measured by today's standards would most assuredly involve personal high achievements such as having seminary or college degrees, being appointed to high positions, being seen on television broadcasts, having large church memberships, having mega ministries, etc.

Some men and women have gravitated to the position of pastor for the sake of being great. The office of pastor brings with it not only great attention, popularity, and responsibility, but also great heartache and much persecution. It behooves one to be called, rather than choosing it as a profession. The heart of a pastor can be deeply bruised and broken.

In Christ's kingdom, greatness is determined by service. He said that the chief (the one who was in charge among them), was to serve the others. Using Himself as an example, Christ said that He came to serve, not to be served, and to give His life as a ransom for many (Mark 45:10).

What a price to pay: your life! How many pastors do you know that have sacrificed their lives for the sheep? Again, thank God for those pastors.

The disciples mistakenly thought that Jesus would free them from slavery to Rome. However, He came to free them from slavery even greater than Rome's—our slavery from sin and Satan. Should Christ's death be in vain? He did not die for His own sake, but for our freedom from the rules and regulations set by man as a means to get to God. He set us free from the bondage of guilt and sin.

The pastor is to be servant to the flock of God. He is to give himself over to the study of the Word of God so that he might teach and train the flock of God to do the work of the ministry. I repeat, pastors are to be servants, beloved; servants of God, servants to the people of God. Too many have lost the spirit of servanthood.

Yes, the pastor represents Christ as he leads the flock of God. His office is an awesome position that should not be taken lightly. Yes, it is a position of honor and the servant of God who holds such a position should be deemed honorable, but the glory must rebound to our Lord and Savior Jesus Christ.

Pastors should not take any glory for themselves, for it is by Christ, in Him, and through Him that they are made able to serve. Leaders should serve as examples of who they are and by example of what they do. They are to endure hardness as good soldiers. They must learn to be content in whatever state they are in; learning to have plenty and to suffer need. God Himself is their enabler and sustainer, their re-reward (rear guard). (See 2 Timothy 2:3; Philippians 4:11; Isaiah 52:12.)

Leaders who are called of God do not have to look out for themselves, the Lord looks out for them. That's called trusting God. It is a hard thing to do if your focus is only on material gain and outward appearances.

Christian leaders are admonished to be as wise as serpents, yet gentle as doves (Matt. 10:16). How many leaders have lost their spirit of contentment? At one time success was defined as being in the will of God, not just about having more; more members, more pews, more stuff.

Honor to Whom Honor Is Due

The teachings from many pulpits today reveal that some pastors are exalted above our Lord Jesus Christ. This error of exaltation introduces confusion into the congregation and results in rebellion. It promotes confusion because it is not biblically sound doctrine to lift a leader up above Christ. Created man should never be lifted up above the Creator God. It causes rebellion because the average believer resents being told he has no voice or point of communication with spiritual leaders, only to obey without question. That is unbalanced teaching. Leaders deserve respect, admiration, and honor. Followers are to esteem them very highly in love for their work's sake (1 Thess. 5:13). A sincere appreciation and support of a leader's Christian labor in God's kingdom is always in order.

No Other *Gods* Before Him

The very first commandment states, "Thou shalt have no other gods before me" (Exod. 20:3). Before God gave the Ten Commandments, He prefaced the list by stating, "I am the Lord thy God, which have brought thee out of the land of Egypt, out of the house of bondage" (Exod. 20:2). If God brings His people out of bondage, out of slavery from sin and Satan, why would He then induce them back into a different kind of bondage, a different kind of slavery, a slavery to man?

God wanted His people to learn to respect and reverence Him. Although people of the land worshipped graven images and false gods, Jehovah (God) was the unique One. He wanted to have first place in the lives of His people then; He wants that now.

When a believer receives the righteousness of Christ and starts to live out that righteousness, it produces a life of transformation and a life of subjection—subjection to all authority, not selective authorities. Romans 13:7 admonishes us to render honor to whom honor is due. We are to honor and pray for all who are in authority over us. That includes our employer and government officials, as well as spiritual leaders. There is no denying this truth. Scripture is clear on this subject. We cannot say we honor God and disrespect other authorities. All authorities are of God—the good ones and the bad ones. Learn to deal with ungodly authorities, they are all around us. Ultimately they must stand before a just God, and we see His justice throughout the history of the world. No one escapes. It is the Christian's responsibility to be subject to authority because when we resist authority, we resist God (Rom. 13:1–9).

Subjection to authority never asks us to exalt that authority above God. Exaltation of man leads back into bondage. Salvation offers freedom from the bondage of sin. We are commanded to "love the Lord thy God with all thy heart, and with all thy soul, and with all thy mind. This is the first and great commandment. And the second is like unto it, thou shalt love thy neighbour as thyself" (Matt. 22:37–39).

Let's keep deity as deity, and man as man. There are several teachings that have surfaced today about Christians being "little gods". Yet when you think about it, many Christians cannot even discern their way out of a paper bag. They cannot believe God enough to heal a headache. How then are they little gods? Where is the Christian's manifested power, his manifested authority?

Some believers profess that they can tread upon serpents and scorpions; that they can run through troops and leap over walls (Ps. 18:29). But the minute tribulation and trouble comes, they turn tail and run. When the pain of turmoil hits, many don't know what to do. Some people then, and only then, run to God for help.

Many unlearned believers actually think they are gods. It's very disappointing to them when their formulas and confessions have no power, and when having faith in their own faith is no longer working. It's a tough world out there. The devil is our enemy, and he's not playing games. He'd love for you to build yourself up on a false belief system that has no real spiritual value, but that is built on clichés and innuendos. Our faith should be directed upward to trusting a God who is able to do anything but fail. It should be built on a relationship with the King of kings and the Lord of lords, Jesus Christ, the anointed One. This relationship is established and grows based on the quality time we spend with Him.

The Bishop

In early Christian history a bishop was the chief priest, ruler, and teacher of one or a number of churches, usually in a specific geographic area. *Bishop* is the word *episkopos* in the Greek, which means "overseer." The terms *bishop* and *presbyter*, or *elder* (Greek: *presbuteros*) were often used interchangeably. Gradually the words acquired more distinct meaning in the church world, with the title of bishop used to designate an overseer of pastors as well as laity.

In Scripture these same Greek words can be translated bishop, pastor, elder, superintendent, and overseer. In the King James Version, 1 Timothy 3:1–13 specifically translates the Greek word *episkopos* to the English word bishop.

Timothy gives us a list of qualifications for a leader or servant who would stand in this office to serve God and His people.

A bishop must

1. be blameless (give no grounds for accusation), but must be above reproach (sinless, no, but walking in integrity);

2. be the husband of one wife;

3. be circumspect (careful);

4. be temperate and self-controlled;

5. be sensible, well behaved, dignified, and lead an orderly, disciplined life;

6. be hospitable, showing love for and being a friend to the believers, especially strangers or foreigners;

7. be a capable and qualified teacher;

8. not be given to wine;

9. not be combative, but gentle and considerate;

10. not be quarrelsome, but forbearing and peaceable;

11. not be a lover of money (an insatiable appetite for wealth and ready to obtain it by questionable means);

12. rule his own household well, keeping his children under control, with true dignity, commanding their respect in every way and keeping them respectful;

13. not be a new convert, or he may [develop a beclouded and stupid state of mind] as the result of pride, [be blinded by conceit, and] fall into the condemnation that the devil [once] did;

14. have a good reputation and be well thought of by those outside [the church], lest he become involved in slander and incur reproach and fall into the devil's trap (1 Tim. 3:1–7, AMP).

Today, the term *bishop* is very popular. It has become more of a title than an office. Too many young men and women of God are striving for this recognition. Somewhere in the midst of our service to God, we have lost the significance of humility and servanthood, and we've started a great pursuit and quest for titles. Our desire to be honored by man here on earth is overwhelming! The Lord has called a number of leaders to stand in the office of bishop, and we are thankful for their success in the ministry of obedience to the Lord. We believe that the Lord has called them to the bishopric, and they are wonderful examples for the rest of us.

A common error in religious Judaism was to regard material wealth as the indicator of God's blessing. Psalm 37, verses 1 through 7, however, tell us that not all wealth is a sign of blessing from God. Some people become temporarily wealthy because of ill-gotten gains. Jesus dealt with this concept when He observed the false spirituality of the Pharisees who were worldly minded.

Christ warned us in the sixth chapter of the Gospel of Matthew not to lay up treasures for ourselves in a worldly sense. Those who do, have their reward. Their desire to be seen of men causes them to lay up treasure to gain the outward attention of men. Some even think this could make them more acceptable to God, as well as man. But this just points to a wrong attitude toward material possessions in the first place. Instead of storing up treasures in heaven, where moth and rust doth not corrupt, seekers of material wealth have accumulated treasures on earth and sold themselves for the praise and accolades of men. Christ's message was clear: He said, "Where your treasure is, there will your heart be also" (Matt. 6:21).

The Deacon

In addition to the fivefold ministry gifts, the deacon is a leader, and servant of the leadership and of the flock of God. Deacons are influential in the church, but many of them have caused havoc in administering their responsibilities. It is very important to look at the scriptures concerning their role in the church. They must be chosen for what they are, not what they have or who they are in the world's eyes. There are "musts" for them as well as for the pastor or overseer.

Chapter 3 of 1 Timothy says: In like manner the deacons must

1. be worthy of respect;

2. not be shifty and double-talkers, but sincere in what they say;

3. not be given to much wine,

4. not be greedy for base gain (craving wealth and resorting to ignoble and dishonest methods of getting it);

5. posses the mystic secret of the faith;

6. be tried and investigated and proved first, then if they turn out to be above reproach, let them serve (as deacons);

7. be worthy of respect and serious, not gossipers, but temperate and self-controlled, (thoroughly) trustworthy in all things, if they are women;

8. be the husbands of but one wife;

9. manage their children and their own households well (vv. 8–13, AMP).

Bad Leaders and the Power of Persuasion

Consider for a moment the following world news events that occurred over the last thirty years:

1. The Peoples Temple Church; James (Jim) Jones, pastor and founder; Jonestown, Guyana, November, 1978; 900 deaths from murders and mass suicide.[2]

2. Branch Davidians, Mt Carmel Complex; David Koresh, founder and leader; Waco, Texas, April, 1993; more than 80 deaths (including 22 children) from a shoot out, siege, fire, murders, and mass suicide.[3]

3. Heaven's Gate, Marshall Applewhite, leader; Rancho Santa Fe, California, March, 1997; 21 women and 18 men (ages 26–72) committed mass suicide.[4]

We all watched the news on television and shook our heads in disbelief, thinking how these things could have happened. Some have gone so far as to blame God for allowing this to take place. They contend that God was unfair and should have spared the lives of the innocent people.

These incidents shocked the nation and caused believers everywhere to say, "I'd never do that! I could never be that naive. No spiritual leader could ever persuade me to take my life. I'm not that foolish." Perhaps you wouldn't go to that extreme. As sad and tragic as they were, the above incidents gave many a wake-up call to be aware of unbalanced spiritual leaders. It is quite evident that sophisticated brainwashing took place in each of those organizations. What tremendous power of persuasion these leaders possessed.

You may not be involved to the degree these poor souls were, but the Bible is filled with warnings concerning following the doctrine of false leaders and teachers. God cares so much for us that He has listed in Scripture qualifications that should be prevalent in the lives of His chosen leaders. A tree is known by the fruit it bears. We should see good fruit.

Please don't think that I am suggesting that leaders should be without flaws or sin themselves—not at all. But somewhere in the heart of men and women they should be allowing God to work and establish a level of integrity, so that He can brag about them and say, as He did of Job, "Have you considered my servant…one who fears God and shuns evil" (Job 2:3, NKJV). There are no perfect leaders. But there are leaders who are perfectly yielded to the Lord for His leading and correction.

The Lord is looking for servants whose hearts are wholly toward Him. One who is not out for selfish gain or popularity, or looking to fulfill a need to feel significant in the eyes of men to the point that he must lord over their lives. Many leaders are provoking God with their attempts to get away with pernicious lifestyles and cunning schemes.

There are too many unhappy and bitter Christians leaving the church because they have been abused, manipulated, and controlled. Some are wandering from church to church searching for a better environment because, in their hearts, they really do want God. They try to find fellowship with Christ in the local church because it is commanded in the Scriptures (Heb. 10:5).

Of course not all leave for that reason. It is evident that some Christians have impure motives. In that case, may God arrest and settle them, and help lead them to a tender loving Christian leader who's after God's own heart.

A Brief Look at the Member's Responsibilities

While God was undoubtedly precise with His instructions to His shepherds, the members also had certain responsibilities designated to them regarding their relationship with their leader. Second Corinthians 1:24 tells us that our shepherd (pastor, servant) is a helper of our joy. The members of the church should therefore:

1.	Count them worthy of double honor	1 Tim. 5:17
2.	Pray for them	Rom. 15:30
3.	Know them and esteem them highly	1 Thess. 5:12–13
4.	Remember them and follow their faith	Heb. 13:7
5.	Support them financially	1 Cor. 9:14

Pastors are divinely ordained by God to represent Him in spiritual authority, not to represent themselves. Christians are to submit to their appointed pastors as the ones who watch for their souls (Heb. 13:17). As pastors follow Christ, we are to follow them. The church should commit themselves to cooperate with their pastors and fully support the vision that God has given them, joining them in spiritual labors for the advancement of God's kingdom.

To love, respect, and follow your anointed and appointed pastor, is to love, respect, and follow Christ.

This summarizes God's plan, God's design, God's order. In this imperfect world, it is still a very good plan.

The Balance

As overseers of God's people, a great responsibility is charged to Christian leaders. Yes, they are to instruct us in righteousness, correct us, teach us the way, reprove, rebuke and exhort us. Through their ministering, the church should grow spiritually, fulfill the purpose of God for their individual lives, and fulfill the vision and purpose of the individual church. If all leaders were led by the Lord Himself, the Christian follower would be much happier and would not be easily deceived by the wiles (deceits and strategies) of the devil.

Christian followers would be well taught and would have a godly example of true leadership. Believers could then recognize the difference between that which is holy and that which is profane, between the clean and the unclean (Ezek. 44:23).

CHAPTER 6

LOOKING BACK TO TODAY

(THE GOOD GUYS VS. THE BAD GUYS)

I F YOU ARE old enough, and if your family could afford a television, you might remember watching certain television series in the 1950s, 1960s and 1970s that were referred to as "cowboys and Indians," or Westerns. They dealt primarily with life in the 1800s, usually in Small Town, USA. They portrayed a simple lifestyle in which the majority of citizens were hardworking farmers, sharecroppers, blacksmiths, dressmakers, general store owners, etc. Every town, it seemed, had a saloon, a sheriff, a doctor, a bank, and at least one all-around good guy or Good Samaritan.

To name a few, there was *The Lone Ranger*, *Roy Rogers*, *Annie Oakley*, and *The Cisco Kid*. In those series the bad guys always wore black hats, rode black horses, had shifty eyes, made cunning remarks, had slick tricks, and were, therefore, easily identified or detected throughout the show. We knew who they were.

The good guys, on the other hand, wore white hats, rode white horses, worked hard for a living, and were fine, upstanding citizens in the community. If the good guys were not yet married, they were considered to be the good catch in town. They often courted one of the pretty young daughters of another fine, upstanding citizen.

On the television series *Gunsmoke*, everybody knew that Marshal Matt Dillon was the good guy, along with Festus his deputy, old Doc the town's physician, and Miss Kitty the owner of the saloon. If Festus, Miss Kitty, or Doc got into trouble, the perpetrator had to deal with Marshal Matt Dillon. The Marshal was clearly the good guy. The bad guy in the picture was clearly the bad guy, and at the end of the story, good won and evil lost.

After watching one of those series you could go to sleep assured that it was good and safe to live in America, even in the wild, wild West. Justice almost always prevailed. We could pretty much rest with confidence in our legal system, and also in the way our minds processed the consequences of right and wrong. Of course this was back in the 1950s, 1960s, and 1970s.

Today at the Movies

Today in many of the movies and television series the bad guys are portrayed as the good guys. The tables have turned and, instead of knowing which one to root for based on their attire and characteristics, we have been duped into rooting for the bad guys.

Think about it; today the bad guys carry the latest state-of-the-art weapons. They have schemes that outmaneuver law and order. If we're not careful, we become sympathetic with them because we have been carefully led to admire them and their lifestyles. Before we know it, we begin to root for them to win against justice and righteousness because we're led to believe that they have been victimized by their environment, or they've been dealt a raw deal.

So, what we have then is the bad guys who out sting the police, the military, the FBI, and the courts. Unfortunately they become the heroes of the story.

Here's another one: *The Godfather* trilogy, which was first made in 1972.[1] One can watch those movies a hundred times and learn something different each time. They have made the movies so real that the characters almost become real people. It's no longer just a fictional story.

Here's the scenario: the Corleone family were criminals for years. The criminal traits ran through the family line. The Godfather, played by Marlon Brando, was a criminal. During his earlier years as a criminal back in the old country, Sicily, his character was portrayed by Robert DeNiro. The Godfather taught his son Santino, called Sonny and played by James Caan, so he was also a criminal. When Sonny was murdered by their enemies (also criminals), then his younger brother Michael Corleone, played by Al Pacino, who had tried to be a good guy, took over and he too became a criminal and the new Godfather, or Don.

In *The Godfather III* Michael died, but he had trained and appointed his nephew (Sonny's illegitimate son) Vincent, played by Andy Garcia, to take over, and he also was a criminal. He became the third Godfather. Somewhere in the midst of the three movies, *The Godfather I, II, and III*, we learned to sympathize with and to applaud the bad guy. It seems we became advocates for their cause. When the criminal Michael died, we felt bad and mourned his death, just like we did when the first Godfather died! You know you did, didn't you!

By the way, who were the good guys in those three movies? Can you name at least two or three good guys, innocent people?

I wonder if we can recognize the subtlety with which our adversary, the devil, has infiltrated our thought processes, to accept the unlovely, to root for the criminal, to admire ill-gotten fame and fortune, to envy the rich and famous, and to applaud those who step on and crush the weak just to get ahead.

Things appear to be so diluted today that we cannot clearly see danger, although it's right under our noses. Will anyone recognize the Antichrist when he appears?

Sadly our youth are trying desperately to emulate the bad guys of today. A good number of them have little or no regard for life or for the belongings of others. Their thinking is distorted and they feel society owes them. We must pray that God will turn their hearts and minds back to what is really holy, what is righteous, and what is sacred.

There Are Good Guys and Bad Guys in the Church, Too

Just like we see in the movies today, the devil is working hard through so many leaders within the church structure that it can be hard to tell the good guys from the bad guys. The same old devil that's on the outside of the church is using the same old tactics on the inside of the church.

The bad guys in the church have learned well that they must disguise themselves. They wear spiritual white hats and ride spiritual white horses, so that they appear to be what they are not. They have learned to dress like, act like, talk like, and preach like true, believing Christians. It's as if they went to acting school and learned how to appear as real Christians.

They've read our books, studied the ministries of early successful Church leaders, imitated our characteristics, and presented themselves before us as called and appointed by God.

They even attend conferences and workshops of successful churches and ministries. They join notable Christian organizations. They establish a reputation of faith and a name in the community amongst the sincere men and women of God.

Clothed in dramatics, a pseudo form of working of miracles and performing wonders, they declare prosperity to all who will do what they say and follow their formulas. They have wittingly duped many of the innocent. The Word of God identifies them as false—pretenders, untrue, wicked, or religious imposters.

Some of them want to be called by the latest status symbol in the house of God, "Bishop," as if the title makes them who they are. Titles can offer respect from the community toward those looking for the praise of men. But God is not impressed with our titles. Thank God for those bishops who are called and anointed by God to stand in that office. We appreciate their work and labors of love in the body of Christ. We give thanks to the Lord for allowing them to serve us.

In the church today we see evidence among these bad guys of what John warned against: the lust of the flesh, the lust of the eyes, and the pride of life. According to John's report, they love the world, but the love of the Father is not in them (1 John 2:15–16). Their lifestyle often reveals a lust for physical pleasure, a selfish desire for seemingly everything they see, and a selfish pride in their personal possessions.

John's instruction leaps out at us again. "Beloved, believe not every spirit, but try the spirits whether they are of God: because many false prophets are gone out into the world" (1 John 4:1).

Not only did the apostle Paul speak consistently in his writings concerning false teachers and false prophets, but Christ also taught His disciples many times on the subject. Rather than discerning others by their outward appearance, that is, what they wear, or what they say with their lips, Jesus said, "Wherefore by their fruits ye shall know them" (Matt. 7:20).

Christ taught that believers were not to expect the majority of people to become true believers. In fact, He said only a few people would find the road that leads to life. Immediately following this truth, Christ also told them to beware of false prophets who would come to them in sheep's clothing (Matt. 7:14–15). He wanted His followers to know that the character and lifestyles of these false prophets would reveal their true identity.

In light of this great truth, it is still amazing that some people will choose to remain ignorant. They will hear what false teachers say, see their wicked deeds, but will not be convinced that they are false. When did actions stop speaking louder than words? Jesus went on to say that some of them will continue doing evil until they stand before Him, at which time He will declare that He never really knew them (Matt 7:23).

As Christians, shall we ignore the warnings of our Lord and Savior Christ Jesus? False prophets and false teachers were prevalent back then, but do we really believe that this fact is no longer a truth today? "But evil men and seducers shall wax worse and worse, deceiving, and being deceived" (2 Tim. 3:13).

My friend, the devil uses the same tricks today on a different group of unsuspecting souls. Why should he change his tricks when they have always worked so well? He has been using them successfully for thousands of years.

Jesus warned us to beware of evil men because they will have a religious sound, but will be motivated by money, fame, or power. What kind of fruit will we see produced from them? In their teaching they will minimize Christ and glorify themselves. We should examine their religious words by their lives.

Good teachers will consistently produce good behavior and high moral character as they become doers of the word they teach, and as they point everyone to our risen Savior, Jesus.

The good teachers are not without sin. But if they err or sin, we are commanded in Scripture to forgive them and to extend the mercy of God unto them. We are never taught by Christ to judge so as to condemn, punish, avenge, damn, or to execute judgment upon them. No! The word *judge* is the Greek word *krino*. Wherever we see false prophets and false teachers exposed in Scripture, we are told to judge (Greek: *anakrino*), which means "to examine, investigate, question or discern" This is an important truth to understand because many of them will accuse you of judging (*krino*) them, but you are only obeying the Word of God by discerning, investigating, or examining their fruit (*anakrino*).

The message from Matthew 7 exposes the corrupt teachers who would deliberately teach false doctrine for selfish gain. By their fruit you shall know them.

God Talks to Ezekiel, Old Testament

Even back in the Old Testament, God used priests and prophets to warn His people about false prophets. Ezekiel was a priest who had been taken captive from Jerusalem to Babylon. God used him mightily to speak to His people and to warn them. Ezekiel's message was directed to the Israelites who had been taken captive, but needed desperately to know and understand that Israel's God was their God in a foreign country as well as at home. However, since they fell consistently to idolatry, Ezekiel had to strongly warn them about the consequences of their disobedience. His message was a message of God's judgment and salvation. God was calling His people to repentance and obedience.

In chapter 22 Ezekiel preaches and demonstrates God's truth as he predicts the approaching siege and destruction of Jerusalem. Read and look carefully as he describes the state of the prophets, priests and other leaders, and their effect on the people of God. See how the leaders lead the people *in* sin and to *commit* sin.

Ezekiel's message from God was to convey to the people their sins and their coming dispersion. It was a hard word to deliver. It was not sugarcoated at all. God was not pleased with His leaders. Today He is still looking for someone to make up the hedge and to stand in the gap before Him for the land.

Failing to keep God's worship pure and holy, the priests became loose and neglected their priestly responsibilities, which were designed to keep God and His holiness before the people.

The leaders were responsible for the moral state of the nation of Israel because God chose them to lead. We can clearly see now, as it was then, that leaders stand in need of much prayer. There are some who are truly anointed vessels of God.

I must also mention the fact that Satan has certain specified attacks and strategies that are designed to destroy God's leaders. It takes a strong man or woman of God to stand in this evil day, just as it did in Old Testament times. No leader should lead on his own, out of his own mind. He must, in all his ways, acknowledge God, that He might direct his paths (Prov. 3:5–6).

For their own sakes leaders need a reliable accountability among their peers and other elders to help them stay upright in moral and spiritual integrity. It is not good for leaders to refuse advice, suggestions, and accountability from others here on earth, stating that they hear only from God in heaven. We should not be "Lone Rangers". God has called us to work together and to support one another. We are to be accountable to each other. Danger lies in wait for an ungovernable spirit.

Paul's Teaching, New Testament

Leaders are charged by God to take heed (take care) for themselves and for all the flock over which the Holy Ghost has made them overseers (Acts 20:28–29). In these verses Paul says that the flock of God had been purchased by the blood of Jesus. He knew that as soon as he left their presence, grievous wolves would come in among them and not care about the flock of God. Grievous wolves come in for one purpose only, to eat, scatter, or devour the flock.

Paul went further to say that among the leaders themselves men would come to the front and say perverse, distorted, and corrupt things in an effort to draw the followers to themselves; perhaps to start a new group, or to get them to follow them out of the safety of their own group. Leaders were, therefore, to be alert and on guard at all times (Acts 20:30–31). We find too often that instead of taking care of themselves and the flock of God, leaders today take advantage of the flock and take away their liberty. They dictate, scorn, criticize, and intimidate God's people. This should not be.

James's Teaching

My brethren, be not many masters, knowing that we shall receive the greater condemnation.

—JAMES 3:1

The Epistle of James sheds another very interesting light on the responsibility of leaders. In chapter 3, verse 1 the word *masters* is used; it comes from the Greek word *didaskalos*, which means "instructor, doctor, teacher." This title includes pastors, church leaders, missionaries, preachers of the Word, or anyone who gives instruction to a congregation. The master (teacher) must understand that no one has a more solemn responsibility than those who teach the Word of God. In the future judgment, Christian teachers will be judged more strictly than other believers.

The Amplified Bible records the same verse this way: "Not many [of you] should become teachers (self-constituted censors and reprovers of others), my brethren, for you know that we [teachers] will be judged by a higher standard and with greater severity [than other people. Thus, we assume the greater accountability and the more condemnation]."

Two other Bible translations state it a little differently. The New American Standard says, "We will incur a stricter judgment." The New International Version says, "We who teach will be judged more strictly." That's pretty plain. Leaders have no right to take their responsibility lightly, not for lucre or for self-gratification. The responsibility is too awesome. We must stand before a Holy God, a just God.

CHAPTER 7

LEGALISM IS LIKE A CANCER

So, what is legalism? We have dedicated this chapter to a discussion on legalism. Before delving into this subject consider a few preliminary concepts.

How do people end up in legalistic organizations? How can people allow themselves to be scorned, dominated, criticized, and intimidated by a religious leader? Conclusions suggest that they must surrender themselves to that leader. Although the individual had to surrender, that decision may have come as a result of the art of manipulation and/or brainwashing by someone skilled or empowered in this area. This empowerment is not an empowerment from our Lord.

When challenged, not many in legalism are willing to admit that they have been brainwashed. This insults their intelligence. As a matter of fact, some are willing to stay in this brainwashed legalistic state rather than admit that they are not there of their own free will, no matter how obvious the situation appears to others.

In a later chapter it will be brought out, as amazing as it may seem, that it is not only ignorant people who are ensnared in legalism.

Legalism is like a cancer, a malignant tumor of potentially unlimited growth that expands by invasion into other parts of the body. Everyone hates cancer. It's something evil that spreads and inwardly leaves a path of destruction. It not only affects the diseased person, but family, friends, loved ones, and others involved in his or her life. They are affected because they care and wish that this awful thing had not happened to someone they care about.

Because legalism can destroy the follower who's directly involved, which in turn affects family members and friends, the process by which we and others can be infected by this cancerlike agent must be understood.

Before tackling the definition of legalism, we first must understand what it means to be brainwashed. Those who have ever been brainwashed shouldn't be too upset. It can happen to the best of people, in a variety of areas of their lives. Read on and see.

Brainwash

Webster's Dictionary definition:

> A forcible indoctrination that induces you to give up your own basic political, social, or religious beliefs and attitudes and to accept someone else's contrasting regimented ideas; persuasion by propaganda or salesmanship.

The leader who operates in this area has a special gift of charisma and finesse. But remember, not everyone who has charisma is out to manipulate.

Still it is amazing how many people insist they cannot be brainwashed. Yet many have fallen prey to a great deal of sales propaganda throughout their lifetime and have been entrapped into financial strongholds, including credit card debts. Think about all those things you didn't intend to buy when you left home, but did because the smooth talking salesperson caught you at a vulnerable time. Desire, coupled with the salesperson's ability to persuade, caused you to yield. Whether this is sophisticated manipulation or not, it's something to think about.

Christians are admonished to "Trust in the Lord with all thine heart; and lean not to thine own understanding. In all thy ways acknowledge him, and he shall direct thy paths" (Prov. 3:5–6). It is evident, however, that many have placed their religious leader as their "Lord". They seem to trust them and what they say, rather than seeking the true and living God.

The Mice Story

The story is told of a laboratory's experiment with mice. The mice were subjected to considerable abuse over a set period of time. Locked in a small cage with limited space the mice were poked, kicked, jabbed, denied food, had water sprayed on them, etc. After subjection to this sort of abuse for a period of time, the door of the cage was opened giving the mice a chance to escape to freedom. To everyone's surprise, the mice went up to the opened door, looked out, and returned to their corner in the cage. They chose to remain in the abusive situation rather than to escape to freedom.

Many of God's people are just like the mice. They choose to remain in abusive situations rather than live under the grace, liberty, and freedom provided by Christ. Perhaps this is because they do not recognize the true voice of the Lord God of heaven.

We consider the voice of our leaders or pastors to be the voice of God, and too often they misrepresent Him. Thank God for the pastors who do not misrepresent Him.

Now, to define "legalism".

Legalism
Webster's Dictionary definition:

> Strict, literal, or excessive conformity to the law or to a religious or moral code; (often which restricts free choice); drawing authority from or founded on law.

A legalist, then, is an advocate or adherent of moral legalism; or one who views things from a legal standpoint. In a nutshell, and for the purpose of defining the word in this writing:

> Legalism is the need to follow the law or a set of man-made rules in order to be, or to feel accepted by God or leaders.

The Book of Galatians discusses this subject strongly and directly because the Christians at Galatia had fallen into legalism. False teachers called Judaizers had brought in a doctrine, which was causing much confusion among the church. Judaizers believed that Gentile believers must come into the church under the same terms that governed the entrance of Gentile proselytes (converts) into Judaism.

Paul learned that these Jewish teachers were unsettling his new converts in Galatia by imposing circumcision and the yoke of the law given by Moses as necessary requirements for salvation and inclusion in the church.

At that time Paul considered legalism a very serious condition which stagnated believers' growth in Christ. It is still a very serious condition today for believers. Paul, therefore, in his letter to the Galatians, used strong language to alert them and to break that stronghold. They had come to Christ by faith, but now were listening to teaching that insisted that they add works of the law to their faith.

The purpose of Paul's letter to Galatia was to emphatically deny that the legal requirements, such as circumcision, under the old covenant had anything to do with the operation of God's grace in Christ for salvation under the new covenant.

Paul also wanted to strongly convey and clearly reaffirm that we receive the Holy Spirit and spiritual life through faith in the Lord Jesus Christ alone, and not by adding the works of the Old Testament law.

So the letter to the church at Galatia has been called the Magna Carta of the early church, a document which constituted a fundamental guarantee of rights and privileges.

The Book of Galatians has become known as the letter of Christian liberty because it explains the nature of our liberty, it helps us to understand how to apply the laws of our liberty, and it emphatically curses the enemies of our liberty. It is literally the corrective solution to anyone who has lost their freedom and entered into bondage. It's right there in the Word of God, dear friend, He wants us to be free.

Faith, Not Legalism

The opposite of living in legalism is to live by faith through the grace that Christ provided. Listen to the strong language Paul used in his efforts to get through to the Galatians:

> O foolish Galatians, who hath bewitched you, that ye should not obey the truth, before whose eyes Jesus Christ hath been evidently set forth, crucified among you? This only would I learn of you, Received ye the Spirit by the works of the law, or by the hearing of faith? Are ye so foolish? having begun in the Spirit, are ye now made perfect by the flesh?
> —GALATIANS 3:1–3

Bewitched is a very strong word! The Galatian Christians were attempting to obey the additional rules that the Judaizers had introduced to them. The Judaizers were like so many today who are afraid to live by grace. They reason in their minds that it's too easy, I must do something to earn my salvation and to feel saved; or they feel that if they don't set high standards and rules to live by, they will live a loose lifestyle and be like other sinners. God forbid that they should be guilty of doing things that other sinners do. If they don't smoke, don't chew, don't curse, and don't do the visible things that they determine is sin, they feel superior.

Are Christians afraid to live and depend on the grace that Christ delivered to the church? Christ is indeed able to keep protecting believers who have committed their lives to Him. He is willing and able to keep them from failing in their Christian walk. His work is first an internal working in the believer's heart. When the believer's heart is wholly His, he will choose to live upright before Him.

The Galatian Christians had become fascinated by the proclamations of the Judaizers. As new converts they had become very unsettled. The false teachers had imposed on them the necessity for them to be circumcised and baptized in addition to faith in Christ. In other words, they taught that they must follow a set of rules to be accepted by God. They had become victims to obeying rules and regulations. As long as they followed the do's and don'ts, they felt religious. When they did not obey the rules they were taught that they did not please God and were still sinners.

This is just where corrupt leaders want believers to be: living by their feelings.

Are all false teachers aware that they are false? Some know what they are doing, others are self-deceived and don't know. Some may be very sincere in what they are teaching, but may be sincerely wrong. It is their motive that must be examined by the Lord. Believers should not judge and condemn them; but Jesus said in Luke 6:44, "For every tree is known by his own fruit." Christians must be fruit inspectors. Their lives may depend upon their accurate assessment of what they are being taught.

As sincere as some false teachers can be, their doctrine can squeeze the life right out of a believer.

Paul's heart ached for the truth to reach these new believers. His letter to the Galatians denied emphatically that there were any "legal" requirements, such as circumcision, under the old covenant, for salvation by grace under the new covenant.

He wanted to make it crystal clear to the Galatian Christians that they received the Holy Spirit and a new spiritual life only through faith in the Lord Jesus, not by keeping any Old Testament law.

Grace Yesterday, Grace Today

Is God's grace the same for us today as it was for the believers in Galatia? Absolutely! Believers receive new life in Christ, not by keeping a set of rules, but through faith in Christ alone.

Circumcision may not be one of the rules that believers are dealing with today, but there are other rules they are trying to follow that are equally binding. They have the same effect. Rules such as: women can't wear make up or cut their hair; women can't wear pants; men can't wear their hair long; Christians can't go to ball games, or indulge in any worldly activity; Christians can't celebrate birthdays.

The list goes on and on, depending on which denomination or fellowship a person is involved with. If they were to leave one fellowship or church for another, they might have to learn a different set of rules in order to be accepted at the new church. Rules, rules, rules! How many of the rules set by man are pertinent to salvation?

When a person tries to live under the law of obedience to rules, they find themselves caught in a multitude of errors. Some people are fairly good at obeying rules to a certain extent and for a period of time, but when their behavior is carefully observed you will probably see a person who is very self-righteous, haughty, stuck-up, and arrogant. These are not desirable character traits.

There is a danger we should consider when a person is focused on obeying the rules. That person begins to tell himself that "because I am obeying the rules":

1.   I am more spiritual than others who are not keeping the rules.

2. My pastor or leader likes me, thinks well of me, favors me, and will soon promote me.

3. God likes me, thinks well of me, favors me, and will soon promote me.

4. I will be a better person and improve my quality of living.

5. People will notice me and will compliment me often for being a good Christian. I will be a great example.

When a believer looks for approval and acceptance from someone he feels is more spiritual than he is, it can entrap him and keep him in bondage to that person. If that leader verbalizes displeasure in him, the person gets out of sorts and wrestles inside to find a way to get back in good with them.

Sometimes believers place the opinion of their leaders over God's opinion. This is wrong. The Word of God is clear to those who are heirs of salvation and joint heirs with Christ. In Romans 8:31 Paul tells us, "If God be for us, who can be against us?" No one's opinion can separate us from the love of God which is in Christ Jesus our Lord (Rom. 8:35).

Elitism

Regrettably, some Christians submit to the distorted authority of false teachers. They often strive to be like them, spiritual and awesome. With this attitude, they add their arrogance to the arrogance of the false teacher, and before you know it, they both are important in their own sight.

An attitude of elitism introduces a powerful spirit of error within any individual. (See Part II for more on the spirit of elitism.) This spirit of error strips the elitist of his freedom in Christ, but he cannot see it. He often measures all other Christians by a standard he has adopted for himself. That standard is one of perfection, super spirituality, and personal significance above other Christians. In his mind everyone else falls short of attaining this same standard. If he is a leader, this attitude assures him that he is a step above his followers. The spirit of elitism is not the spirit that Christ would have believers to walk in.

Yoke of Bondage

Paul warned against the false teachers who took away the liberty and freedom from sincere Christians by requiring them to follow a set of rules. Paul described it as putting "a yoke of bondage" on them (Gal. 5:1). He did not yield to these false teachers for even a moment, because he wanted the gospel to continue to be preserved in its purity before the Galatians.

> Come unto me, all ye that labor and are heavy laden, and I will give you rest. Take my yoke upon you, and learn of me; for I am meek and lowly in heart: and ye shall find rest unto your souls. For my yoke is easy, and my burden is light.
> —MATTHEW: 11:28–30

A yoke is something that unites or binds. It is also a heavy wooden harness, a bar or a frame by which two draft animals are joined at the heads or necks for working together. The yoke is used on oxen so they can pull loads.

Laden comes from the word *lade,* which means "to put a load or burden on." A "heavy laden" animal has a big load to pull. A person who is heavy laden may be burdened with sin, excessive demands of religious leaders or oppression, persecution, or weariness in their search for God. Jesus came to free people from these burdens. Jesus also promises acceptance without the do's and don'ts. He offers unconditional love, restoration, healing, and peace with God. Christians do not have a license to live any way they want. However, they do have the freedom to let the Holy Spirit sanctify them as they grow in His grace. As a Christian sees the light, he walks in it; as he grows, he changes.

A covenant relationship with God changes meaningless sweat and toil into spiritual productivity and purpose. Christians should continually strive for that personal relationship with Him. It bears repeating again, believers do not need to obey rules for acceptance. There is enough evidence in the Bible that says we don't (Rom. 5:8–10).

Since believers are acquitted, made righteous, and brought into a right relationship with God by the shed blood of Jesus Christ, they can be assured that they will be saved by Him from the indignation and wrath of God. They need not add their own or anyone else's "rules" to be insured they are saved. Otherwise, Christ's death at Calvary was not enough to atone for their sins.

How many voices like the apostle Paul's are available and sounding loud to guard the purity of the gospel among new believers today? How is it that so many are falling captive to this cancer-like agent called legalism? It spreads very quickly and it is very destructive.

Thousands of believers feel they are spiritual just because they follow the rules of do's and don'ts set by their leaders. Many of them are condemning other believers who do not follow those same rules.

Christ came that we might have abundant life. He came to set captives free, not to put us in bondage. He came not to condemn the world, but that the world through Him might be saved (John 3:17). When the Holy Spirit is leading and Christ is the Chief Shepherd, believers will have liberty, not bondage. They will have cooperation, not competition. They will give God all the glory, and not lift their Christian leaders above God.

Godly principles and guidelines from the Word of God are not being eliminated. No one can live a successful Christian life without obeying the Word of God. I am not advocating that there are no rules, no principles by which Christians are held accountable to obey. What is important is the preeminence of the grace of God in the life of every believer who yields to His sanctification and within this process sanctifies himself also.

In Galatians 5:22 Paul proclaims the fruit that will be evident as the Holy Spirit reigns in the believer's life. When the believer's whole life is under the dominion of love, bondage to self is no longer possible. The plan of the enemy is to keep all believers from believing and receiving the love of God through Christ. He wants to keep them searching and working to find and feel God's love.

As a born again believer, if you are constantly trying to be accepted, you never really come to a place of rest. You never come to a place of knowing that you are accepted in the beloved (Eph. 1:6). It is by grace that we are saved through faith, and even that is not of ourselves. It is the gift of God, not by our works, lest any man should boast (Eph. 2:8–9).

The moment Christians make anything other than faith supreme, they establish a rite. A rite is a prescribed form or manner governing the words or actions for a ceremony. Christians are not called to grace only to live out a ceremony of religious rules and actions. They are called to life in Christ, not by their works of righteousness.

PART II

WARNING SIGNALS

A SCRIPTURAL FOUNDATION

CHAPTER 8

THE VULNERABLE AND THE INNOCENT

U NDER THE RULE of the Pharisees and Sadducees, the people of God labored continually and never found rest. The Pharisees could not secure them in their relationship with a Holy God, because they did not know God. Christ was bold enough to tell them, if they knew God, they would have recognized Him, Jesus, as being sent from God (John 5: 37–38).

New babes in Christ are unlearned in the things of God and can easily be led into bondage, especially the sincere and innocent ones. You see, sincerity of heart does not make them exempt from the schemes, wiles, and temptations of the devil. It may, on the other hand, make them even more vulnerable.

Christians must pray without ceasing and study to show themselves approved unto God, as they rightly divide the word of truth. False teachers and preachers were prevalent during the times we read about in the Scriptures, and they are prevalent today as well.

In Hosea 4:6 the Lord said His people are destroyed because they don't know Him.

What will false teachers and preachers offer believers today? They will only lead us into a state of confusion, separate us from our loved ones, separate us from other Christians, and require us to adhere to a list of their rules and regulations.

Some teachers have gone as far as ordering the dietary habits, the social life, and the physical appearance as well as the economic, political, and religious practices of their followers. It is necessary for all Christians to be aware of their schemes and wiles. There are signals that warn us about falling into traps set by false leaders. What makes a person yield to those traps and schemes, anyway?

Many people are very vulnerable in relationships that they think offer them recognition, esteem, significance, position, or a title with a little bit of power. Sadly, our naïve selfish desires can lead us straight into bondage.

If you want to be seen and praised of men, if you feel the need to be out front, if you crave the kind of attention that makes you feel important, you are a prime target to be drawn into bondage and control.

It is ironic, however, that people can be very sensitive to any mention or insinuation that their involvement in a controlling relationship could be hazardous. Have you ever tried to talk to someone about it? They flat out refuse to believe it. They will even disassociate with friends and loved ones who try to warn them of the potential consequences of their involvement. If the controller discovers that someone is speaking against their relationship with them, they can become hostile too.

The Costly Price of Involvement

Broken marriages and broken relationships are a very expensive price to pay for a person's right to stay involved in a bondage situation because they refuse to listen, or even investigate what is being said.

What most people desire is a healthy, loving attitude toward life and living. Yet thousands are ensnared by their own desire to belong to an organization that gives them what they feel is significance outside of fundamental Christianity. Perhaps they were once hurt by another Christian. If so, this often closes the door for sincere Christians, but opens the door for bondage and control by others who are self-serving.

The warnings found in this section are only intended for those who are looking for *balance* in their lives. It is for those who want to live a free, wholesome, and abundant life, free from the rudiments of this world system and free from the snare of preying false prophets and teachers. It is for those who want to have a loving, wholesome relationship with Christ Jesus, our Lord. A relationship with Him is far more rewarding, far more fulfilling than a relationship with a false teacher. He will never cause you to be ashamed. Jesus never fails!

A Word About the Branch Davidians

Previously, we mentioned a few bad leaders in the news. Let's go back to one of them, David Koresh, former leader and founder of the Branch Davidians, a religious group located in Waco, Texas. David Koresh thought he was an angel and an agent of God. The U.S. government thought he was a criminal who physically and sexually abused many of his followers.

Approximately eighty followers died with Mr. Koresh in a fire during an FBI assault on their compound. Several of David Koresh's followers were not at the compound when the mass loss of lives occurred. Yet, in one news clip, an elderly lady was still swearing to her death that he (David Koresh) was a good man of God, and did his people no harm.[1] She honored David Koresh as if he were God, though he led many to their deaths.

Like the Branch Davidians, people will fight to the death to defend their involvement in an organization that keeps them in bondage and denies them liberty and the pursuit of happiness outside of their group. On the outside looking in, we scratch our heads and say, "What's the matter with them? Can't they see how crazy those people are?"

The answer for some would be, "No, they really can't see." For others it would be, "They don't want to see."

You can almost hear them saying, "Leave me alone and don't confuse me with any facts."

To their detriment they continue in these relationships until the consequences are devastating. Sadly that devastation usually involves not just their own lives, but the lives of their family, friends, and loved ones who share their pains as well as their joys. It brings troubled oppression into their lives.

The Need for Warning Signals

Warning signals are a vital part of our culture and society. They inform us of dangers past, present, and future. We see them everywhere: on the outside and inside of buildings, on sidewalks, in the streets, in parks, on recreational grounds, in our homes, automobiles—literally everywhere we work, play, rest, and exist.

Warning signals are present for our protection, to keep us from running into danger or getting into unpleasant or undesirable situations. We are not only alerted, but also warned of the mild to severe and sometimes deadly consequences, should we persist. We obey and heed them because we believe those who have gone before us to test this area and that they have already determined there really is danger ahead.

Many of us would not dare cross the line to explore whether the warning is real or not. We trust those signals, don't we? They are sometimes inconvenient and a nuisance, but we pretty well abide by them. A percentage of skeptics out there will occasionally challenge a warning. They soon learn, however, that there was a reason for that warning signal.

When a warning is given it is usually given in plain but strong language. They are written in big bold letters because we want people to see them. Here are a few of them that we see almost everywhere:

CAUTION!

BEWARE OF DOG!

DANGER!

KEEP OUT!

STOP!

NO TRESPASSING!

POISON!

IRRITANT, MAY CAUSE BLINDNESS!

RAILROAD CROSSING!

HOT, DO NOT TOUCH!

DO NOT INJEST INTERNALLY!

CAUTION, CONTENTS MAY BE
HAZARDOUS TO YOUR HEALTH!

Bible Warnings

The Bible is full of warnings too. We are cautioned about our life-style, the people we enter into relationships with, the things we get involved in, our motives and attitudes, and we are also warned about our adversary, the devil. With this in mind let's review a few warning signals and red flags concerning our involvement in legalism. Four warnings are given, but there are significant details throughout that reveal the strategies used to make them effective.

The language is strong, as warning signs are meant to be. They are there to save your life, to protect you from danger. Stop! Examine them carefully with God's Word and proceed cautiously, so that you can make the right decision for your own personal welfare and the welfare of your loved ones.

CHAPTER 9

WARNING SIGNAL NO. 1: ELITISM

One of the visible signs of leaders moving in legalism is that they have an exalted assessment of themselves and the organization they have founded.

Whether they are self-appointed, elected, or have actually been appointed by a presbyter, this characteristic will be prevalent. It will be prevalent even if they originally began their work as a humble, submissive, anointed, and spirit-filled leader. They may have started out walking in integrity and responded to a real call of God on their lives, only to have fallen later in disobedience as Saul, first King of Israel, did. Saul fell from grace and from the favor of God because, although he started out right, he became prideful, egotistical, disobedient to God, jealous, and abusive of his delegated power.

Legalistic leaders are often very charismatic and will not hesitate to proclaim their exclusive revelations, dreams, visions, and divine appointment from Almighty God.

They will not hesitate to let the world know that God has chosen no other but him or her to do a special work in the earth.

He operates with a spirit of pride, conveying his greatness in subtle ways to convince unsuspecting souls that he really is the one and only. This pride is motivated by the devil. This leader is skilled at keeping himself elevated in the hearts and minds of his followers.

He is exalted above Christ in the hearts of the people. Followers will mention Christ, but will give praise, thanks, and admiration to their leader for any accomplishments in their lives. If questioned, this leader will emphatically deny that he has commanded the people to honor him above Christ, but it is definitely an unspoken command communicated in countless teaching techniques.

Selfishness is evident in that this elite leader is only interested in advancing his own ideas, his own program, and his own growth. He is not as interested in the well-being and growth of his followers, though he may claim otherwise. It's all about his plan, his vision. When necessary he will institute something that will have the outward appearance of being for the followers. On careful examination it all leads back to his own personal advancement. Have you ever received a gift from someone who got a bigger kick out of giving the gift than you did in receiving it? Sometimes the gift is really for them, not you.

When a member displays a sign of discontentment, he will temporarily pacify him. He gives him enough attention to bring him back in line. If that doesn't work, the member will most likely be ousted. Some kind of rejection will follow. He only wants people on his team that applaud him continually. No one can disagree with him.

This leader runs a totalitarian organization. He is solely and absolutely in charge. He is accountable only to God in heaven. Because he prays and seeks the face of God continually, he feels God is the only one he needs to be accountable to. He is married to the Lord and sold out to God, he says. He is above reproach. God corrects him, and no one else. His peers can certainly offer solutions and corrections to obvious problems or concerns, but that's it. No direct confrontation or challenges are permitted.

If a Christian aligns himself with this organization, most likely they too have, or will become elite in their own estimation. They are carefully taught that they are special because they are aligned with the best. Their total loyalty and obedience to the leader, the vision, and the organization is expected. Nothing less will be tolerated. They have been especially chosen by God to do a work in the earth which no one else is doing.

With this attitude it is evident to all around them that pride has crept in. Many followers do not know to what degree they are lifted up in pride. Family members and other balanced Christians can clearly see their conceitedness. It is not hard to detect; they can see it simply by observing their fruit. Relationships have been breeched with family and friends because it is almost impossible to hide this spirit of pride.

The projected attitude is, "We're the best; no one else can compare; we have the solutions that people have searched a lifetime to find."

Somewhere along their spiritual journey they have been blinded by that spirit of elitism. It is an ugly spirit. It is the spirit of the devil and is repulsive to others.

Such attitudes usually originate in the leader. The game the devil has invited others to play is called *Follow the Leader*. It will lead a person into bondage and take them to a depth of pride that isolates them from others outside of their group.

In fact, their desires will change and they will only want to associate with those who believe like them, and with those who are members of their group. They will eat, play, work, and live with only members of the group. Their entire life will be consumed in the group. If that happens they limit their growth and maturity only to where they are and what they can impart in each other. One person said, "I don't need what they can't provide. How tragic."

Curtis Fallbrook's Story

In Chapter 1 we introduced Curtis, a believer who found what he thought was a place of worship suited for him, The Mission Church. If you remember, most of Curtis' friends had joined and were now happily pursuing the good teaching offered there.

Curtis also got involved and did his best to become a part. As mentioned earlier, he told the Mission's pastor that he felt a call to preach the gospel. He was ready to get involved and to do whatever was necessary to start the process of fulfilling that call. However, after trying hard for twelve months to fit in, Curtis left the Mission Church. After seeking the Lord for direction, he realized that it was not right for him to be a member there even though his friends fit in quite well.

The Lord directed Curtis's path to another fellowship where Curtis enjoyed the liberty and freedom in Christ he sought.

He did not understand why the Mission Church wasn't right for him until he got involved in the new church. The freedom and liberty in Christ was unmistakably different. The joy of the Lord was prevalent and Christ was not only exalted, but glorified continually.

Curtis did not want to be overly critical of the Mission Church, especially since he had so many friends attending who were very satisfied. When questioned about his leaving, he was careful not to sow seeds of discord among those who were still attending there and who were very happy (Prov. 6:19). He merely indicated that the Lord had something different for him.

At the new fellowship, things were clear in his mind and in his heart, while at the Mission he was often confused about doctrinal teaching. He noticed a big difference in the two churches. The spirit of the fellowship at the new assembly was characteristically distinct from the Mission Church. Although he moved cautiously into this new church, he was soon quite elated about being there.

One of the first things he noticed was a freedom of thought and expression. What liberty! He had not realized the confining presence at the Mission that had limited his ability to freely express what he was thinking. Here there was nothing confining him. The freedom allowed him to ask questions so that he could get clarity and understanding.

When he expressed himself incorrectly, the corrections he received were without condemnation and guilt attached to them. He had not enjoyed this liberty at the Mission Church.

Curtis also observed that Christ was preeminently exalted at the new church, not the pastors and elders. Although the pastor and elders were honored and esteemed highly in love for their labor and work in the ministry, Jesus was always the focus of attention. (See 1 Thessalonians 5:13.) There were no predominate elitists in the leadership. No big "me's" and little "you's." God alone got the glory!

In addition, the pastor at the new church was clearly shepherding the flock, leading God's people in the vision that the Holy Spirit had directed. This was evident. It was not the pastor's own personal and private agenda being carried out for his own fame, recognition, and prestige.

Also, the pastor functioned with a board of elders who worked with him and supported the vision of the church. There was no absolute authority that dictated to the staff and viewed them in an ungodly, subordinate manner. Although there were challenges that the leadership faced, they appeared to be handled in meekness with respect and in love (Gal. 6:1).

Curtis also noticed that his personal conversation with the pastor at the new fellowship was very positive and encouraging. When this pastor was told of Curtis' call to preach the gospel, he helped Curtis set up a series of short-term and long-term training goals and to schedule classes that would promote his gifts, talents, and his potential. Some of the suggested classes were to be held at the church, and others were courses offered at other reputable learning institutions.

For the first time Curtis felt he had a mentor that would help him reach his goal and fulfill his God-given purpose. His pastor was someone who was not intimidated by his call to the ministry, and who did not have a need to belittle him and hold him back. Curtis was excited. He realized it was a long road ahead of him, but he saw that it was attainable. He was well on his way to experiencing the spiritual growth he wanted.

Being at the right place, under the right leadership, at the right time of his life, Curtis saw clearly where God was taking him.

That uncomfortable feeling that Curtis had at the Mission Church was for a reason. His friends had an exalted view of their leadership and also of themselves. But God had something better for Curtis. His heart was after the Lord. He listened to that still, small voice inside of him prompting those warning signals.

Even though his friends were content to march to a different beat, Curtis was his own man. He was neither a follower of the crowd, nor a man pleaser. His friends were sure they were in the right place, and perhaps for them, they were. But Curtis knew something was not right there for him. His spirit would not allow him to unreservedly submit in a legalistic environment.

Curtis listened to the voice of the Holy Spirit as He led him out of a place of bondage, into a place of truth, grace, and balance. Hallelujah! Thank God Curtis heeded that warning signal and escaped misery and unrest.

This concludes the wonderful deliverance of Curtis Fallbrook. You can read one final note about him in Part III: The Way Out—Transition and Restoration, Chapter 16, Grace.

The Lord Detests a Proud Look

In the sixth chapter of Proverbs we find a number of practical warnings and insights on daily living. Profound and strong proclamations are made throughout the chapter, but beginning at verse 16 we find a climax to the instructions of verses 12 through 15 about a deceitful, treacherous and wicked person.

> These six things doth the Lord hate: yea, seven are an abomination unto him: a proud look, a lying tongue, and hands that shed innocent blood, An heart that deviseth wicked imaginations, feet that be swift in running to mischief, A false witness that speaketh lies, and he that soweth discord among brethren.
>
> —PROVERBS 6:16–19

The above scripture describes a sinful attitude which is shown by a proud look. This look reveals that an inward error is manifesting outwardly. How sad it is that most who are proud and look down on others are not aware of it. Grace recipients should not be named among them.

In the above scripture, the word *proud* means "to exalt oneself, to magnify oneself, to be high, lofty, or exalted." Proverbs puts this Hebrew word *gaon* (translated *proud*) together with arrogance, evil behavior, and perverse speech. While reading this sixth chapter of Proverbs, you get the sense of haughtiness, conceitedness of ourselves, and contempt of others. It starts out talking about a sluggard (a lazy person) and continues on through the verses describing an evil wicked person. God hates this attitude because, in many instances, it is the root cause of many other sins.

When pride has grown to the point that it shows on one's countenance, it becomes evident that the person has overvalued himself. When he has overvalued himself, he undervalues others around him. It is obvious why God does not like this characteristic. He is a God of love. He has not valued anyone above another. He values and loves us all.

If a person walks in this attitude too long, it can become a spirit of pride. Pride is the very nature of Satan. Too much pride will destroy a person.

Most people struggle with some measure of pride. We are taught as children to be proud; proud of our accomplishments, proud of our heritage, proud of our possessions, etc. When we become adult Christians we are taught that pride is something we must shun. We need a balance in our understanding about it. We should be confident in Christ, but we must beware of taking too much pride in ourselves and our accomplishments. Without Christ we can do nothing.

New creatures in Christ must put on Christ, since we are baptized into Him. We are only transformed from any spirit of pride by the awesome work of the Holy Spirit as we yield to His work in our lives.

The Balance

> For I say, through the grace given unto me, to every man that is among you, not to think of himself more highly than he ought to think; but to think soberly, according as God hath dealt to every man the measure of faith.
>
> —ROMANS 12:3

Paul's caution here is warranted, since so many Christians today are confused about the difference between confidence in Christ and pride. Believers are never to appear arrogant and haughty, but they are to exemplify Christ in all that they do. He is love. As Christians we are now living a transformed life. We are no longer walking in darkness, but in the light. Our minds should be renewed by daily reading and meditating on the written Word of God.

We are to exercise self-control and live with a sober, reasonable assessment of ourselves. We are not to have attitudes of superiority.

A transformed life is lived in a state of humility. Believers should continually subdue the tendency to be prideful.

You can recognize this warning signal when it struts itself among the children of God. Do not be lured into its trap by excusing their behavior. There is freedom from this bondage of elitism, pride, and a haughty spirit. A remarkable deliverance awaits those who are willing and obedient. They can choose to obey the Scriptures, walk with God, and reap the benefits of a happy, successful Christian heritage of God's amazing grace.

CHAPTER 10

WARNING SIGNAL NO. 2: POWER AND CONTROL

O NE PERSON'S ABILITY to usurp power and control in another person's life has been an existing problem for years. It is manifested in marriages, families, businesses, and also in the church. Although the Bible is explicit about how leaders should treat those who are under their authority, the problem of exercising inappropriate power and control still exists in the pulpit and pews today.

This problem must be confronted. This excessive display of power and control surrounds us. Husbands control wives. Wives manipulate their husbands. Parents exercise ungodly power and control in their children's lives. Organizations, public and secular, have leaders who control their employees by manipulating them to get what they want. This is a real problem in the world today.

Can a balanced life be obtained today—one that is free from the bondage of manipulation and excessive power and control? If we are the perpetrators, can we stop manipulating others and controlling them to get what we want? If we are the victim, how can we recognize when we have been under the control of another and how can we get out from under that control? The real questions are: Do you want to be free? Do you want to be balanced?

In this dysfunctional world, we have a God-given right and admonition to guard ourselves against the threat of wickedness. The Bible tells us: "Beloved, believe not every spirit, but try the spirits whether they are of God: because many false prophets are gone out into the world" (1 John 4:1).

John reminds Christians that the Holy Spirit dwells in us and, as such, we should be led by that same Spirit (1 John 3:24, 4:13; Rom. 8:14). He knew there were false prophets who claimed to be spiritual leaders. How can we know the difference? John and Paul both warn against believers accepting from the false teachers things that are contrary to what they had already received from the teachings of the apostles (2 John 7–10; Gal. 1:8–9). Today, we must rely on the Word of God.

We can learn from this warning too. We can ask ourselves a few soul searching questions about a fellowship:

1. Are they teaching fundamentally (basic) sound (solid and stable) doctrine?

2. Are their teachings and their own lifestyles promoting growth, maturity, and freedom in Christ?

3. Are membership guidelines and principles sound and void of secrecy?

After a teaching session we can ask:

4. Am I confused or clear on what was taught?

5. Am I feeling any shame or guilt, or do I feel spiritual conviction, forgiveness, and hope for the future?

6. Am I free to ask challenging questions?

John says believers are to try the spirit of the teachers. This means we are to check them out by a standard that never changes: the Word of God. Unfortunately many Christians have become uninterested in reading the Word of God for themselves. They are more willing to accept someone else's interpretation of Bible doctrine by only listening. They bring their Bibles to meetings and open them while the reader reads, but seldom pick them up at home to "study, to show thyself approved unto God, a workman that needed not to be ashamed, rightly dividing the Word of truth" (2 Tim. 2:15).

This could be the reason why so many are easily deceived and led into bondage and captivity. If you are in this situation, a controlling leader can count on you *not* studying for yourself. He counts on the fact that his will be the only voice that will be heard. He knows he can interpret the Word of God anyway he chooses to suit his purpose, and it will not be questioned or countered. He is counting on the fact that you are not even going to listen to or pay attention to the voice of the Holy Spirit inside of you—that still small voice whispering warnings. This is the point at which you are most vulnerable. He can then proceed to exercise absolute control over your life. He can use techniques aimed at controlling your thought process and eventually alter your personality. That's deep, but it's real.

If you are a sincere person, the controlling leader knows this. He knows just what to do and how to treat you to keep you where he wants you—in submission to him. If you are really sincere, most likely your desire is to be honest and upright continually. You want to be pleasing to God. This is a prime candidate for the legalistic teacher.

For instance, to secure your relationship with him, the controller will often say exactly the right thing to make you think he is also sincere. He compliments your sincerity, whether he operates in that belief or not. He must keep you confident and convince you that he can relate to where you are.

If a controller gains your confidence, submission to him or his ideas is not something he would have to fight for, you will do it automatically. If this leader can win your confidence, he has won you, the person. The ultimate purpose is to get you to submit of your own free will. It's not a point of winning the person, it's winning your confidence. Your confidence is won as he begins to say what you like to hear and do what you like to do.

If you are a person that constantly seeks God, he will say godly things in your presence and about how to seek Him. If you are a person who's in the business world, he will say things about the business world all the time. If you're into computers, it's computer language. He makes you feel he needs your expertise in your field of interest. He is skilled at making you think, at first, that you are desperately needed by him. He wins you by flattery, not by genuine interest in you as a person.

By the way, I certainly do not want to confuse the skill to lead by control and manipulation with sound Christian leadership skills given by God. Abraham, Isaac, Jacob, Moses, Joshua, Gideon, and many others in the Bible were God's leaders. They did not have to manipulate people to get them to follow. They had the ability to lead because of the call and giftings of God in their lives. Thank God for His called-out leaders who lovingly guide the people of God to fulfill God's purpose in the church. They lead by godly example and by obeying the Spirit of God.

Ungodly manipulators and controllers lead by their fleshly abilities. They are full of false promises and have learned what it takes to get people to follow them unconditionally. Likely they are not novices in that arena. Even if they've just started as a leader over a group, you can look back at their childhood and see the traits and abilities that were already there to manipulate and control others.

Leaders are born, and are either infiltrated by the Holy Spirit or by an ungodly spirit.

Skilled manipulators can control you from a distance, even when you're not in their presence. They pull your strings long-distance, because their voices are ever present in your thoughts. You learn what they like and dislike, what they will accept and will not accept. You become so committed to them that even out of their presence, you obey their voice. You learn that when you're back in their presence you confess your sins and your actions while you were outside of their presence. Confession is a requirement to be a part of the group. You don't realize it, but your confessions are necessary so that you can be controlled. Controllers must know where your thoughts are so that they can guide them in the direction they want.

Deceivers insinuate things that they want to take place, or attitudes they want you to adopt. Sometimes they do not come right out and say things because, if something goes badly, they do not want to be tied to having initiated it. They would rather have you believe that it was your idea, you thought it up, and you're responsible. Their insinuations and their overtones are very strong. They know what they are doing. As the follower you end up catching the overtones and making the statement. That way, the leader can always make a counter decree that it was your idea and you said it, when all the time you're doing exactly what they have manipulated you to do. If something fairs well, they then want all the credit for it, of course.

Susan's Story

Remember Susan Summerstone? Her story was introduced to you in Chapter 1. It was a spirit of power, control, and guilt that temporarily crippled her life. Susan abruptly quit attending her local church because she was not sure what was happening to her. Susan had internal struggles stemming from her past that were now posing serious issues for her at the local church she was attending.

Everyone, like Susan, has a past. No one was born saved. All come to Christ as sinners. We must be transformed by the renewing of our minds. This is part of the function of local churches to make disciples, to perfect the saints. This is done by the teaching of sound doctrine to souls who come into the church to be taught and by persevering with them.

When the church you join for discipleship is legalistic, true discipleship in Christ is not guaranteed. Your concentration will not be on pleasing the Lord, but on pleasing your leaders.

Legalists operate in power, control, and guilt. They have little or no tolerance for your inadequacies and your insufficiencies. They need you to do what they tell you to do, when they tell you to do it. You must be available according to their schedule, and useful to the group when they need you. They do not have time for your internal struggles or problems. They usually tell you to "grow up, and get over it."

A Demand for Perfection

This is exactly what Susan was told by her spiritual leaders. When that control maneuver moved in on her, she didn't know what hit her. She was overpowered by the strength of manipulation, control, guilt, and a demand for perfection.

Once you're taught a principle, the legalists expect you to obey and follow their every command. In their minds, this is the key to your development and the key to your success: total obedience and submission to their authority.

Susan was pressured to perform. The duties and responsibilities assigned to her had become overwhelming. Other things were also overwhelming her. Undoubtedly the Holy Spirit was sanctifying her on the inside. It was necessary for Him to uproot some things so that she could be ready to move on to the next level of spiritual growth.

Only the Holy Spirit knows when He is ready to wash and cleanse us. We must be available when He summons us. The following scripture bears this out.

> To every thing there is a season, and a time to every purpose under the heaven: A time to be born, and a time to die; a time to plant, and a time to pluck up that which is planted; A time to kill, and a time to heal; a time to break down, and a time to build up; A time to weep, and a time to laugh; a time to mourn, and a time to dance; A time to cast away stones, and a time to gather stones together; a time to embrace, and a time to refrain from embracing; A time to get, and a time to lose; a time to keep, and a time to cast away; A time to rend, and a time to sew; a time to keep silence, and a time to speak; A time to love, and a time to hate; a time of war, and a time of peace.
>
> —ECCLESIASTES 3:1–8

It was Susan's season of healing and restoration. She sensed that summons very strongly in her spirit. However her leaders took precedent over her life in the church and out of the church. She was not readily available to seek the Lord.

Did she disobey the Spirit? Yes, in order to obey her leaders. She felt pressure and conflict. Her church leaders continued to control her activities. There could be no conflict with family and personal matters. It was understood that church always came first; it was her duty to the Lord. Susan was told that her church was God; therefore the church must be first. She felt pressure to come in line with what they taught. Her own personal issues would have to be put on hold. The guilt she experienced from that pressure was enormous. It was the straw that broke the camel's back, and the straw which caused her to spontaneously quit.

God did a tremendous work on the inside of Susan during the time she was away from her church. After the Holy Spirit's cleansing, she felt so good inside that she returned to the same local assembly. She felt restored and whole again. Little did she know that she returned to another level of bondage in power and control. The guilt was magnified. The leaders never fully trusted her again. She was allowed back into their fold, but things were not the same as before.

Susan's restoration was short lived because she failed to recognize the strong warning signals from her inner man. She did not understand that she was bound by legalism. In her quest to be accepted by her spiritual leaders, she fell back under that same bondage. She stayed for several years and grew more miserable than she was the first time. She got more deeply entangled in legalism as her life continued in that church. Can God deliver Susan a second time?

Read the conclusion of her story in Part III, Chapter 14, Soul Ties and Fantasy Bonding.

The Balance

Then said Jesus to those Jews which believed on him, If ye continue in my word, then are ye my disciples indeed; And ye shall know the truth, and the truth shall make you free.

—JOHN 8:31–32

Stand fast therefore in the liberty wherewith Christ hath made us free, and be not entangled again with the yoke of bondage.

—GALATIANS 5:1

The words of Jesus and Paul ring true—loud and clear. The remedy to being under this bondage of power and control is to continue in the Word of God and stand fast in that liberty wherewith Christ has made us free. That is balance.

In the beginning verses of our first reference scripture above, John chapter 8, the scribes and Pharisees brought a woman who was caught in adultery to Jesus, to see if He would follow the law of Moses in dealing with her. Once again the Savior is challenged, but handles Himself explicitly by forgiving the sinner and teaching a valuable lesson to all.

Continuing on in verse 12, Jesus describes Himself as the light of the world and assures all who would follow Him that they will not walk in darkness but will have the light of life. Then in verses 31 and 32, He offers comfort to some of the weaker Jews who believed in Him. His message: keep obeying me and you will know the truth and this truth that you know will set you free.

It is very important for all of us to continue in His teachings. A characteristic of true followers was to continuously obey what they had been taught by their teacher. Continuity and obedience constitute growth. Truth will take root and the believers are grounded. The result: they are set free.

The Book of Galatians is written by Paul to the churches at Galatia. Liberty and grace are discussed throughout each chapter. Paul's concern for these churches stems from the activities of the Judaizers who were teaching the new Gentile believers that they needed to conform to the Law of Moses, even after the death, burial, and resurrection of Jesus Christ. They were legalistic.

The Judaizers were religious leaders too. They sounded good and knowledgeable. But their doctrine would take the people of God from living in grace back into the bondage of trying to obey the Law of Moses. It was necessary for Paul to stamp out this spirit of legalism. His preaching on liberty and grace was so strong that it carried the power to win the new converts back to Christ.

We read a very powerful argument from Paul as he tries to set forth the difference between grace and the law, between faith and works, and between the spirit and the flesh. Why go back to bondage? Why not stand fast in this freedom and liberty once delivered to us?

Christendom is infiltrated today by legalism, ritualism, and materialism. We are not better because of it. Our pulpits and pews scream for balance. No one who has the mind of Christ wants to be in bondage. It is true that some are more submissive to bondage techniques than others. Some would prefer that someone else would do their thinking and make decisions for them. All they would have to do is obey. If they obey what they're told, they feel saved.

The will of God is that we all might grow up in Christ and no longer be children, tossed to and fro. We should desire sincere spiritual milk so we can grow into the fullness of our salvation (1 Pet. 2:2). The New Living Translation says we should "cry out for this nourishment" as a baby cries for milk.

Boundaries

Although our New Testament commands us to obey those who have the rule over us, we are expected by the Holy Spirit to use wisdom in our submission. There are boundaries we should respect and demand in our own lives, as well as in the lives of others. We set those boundaries according to the leading of the Holy Spirit and the inspired, rightly divided Word of God. We are required by Scripture to yield to one another in the fear of God and to esteem all leaders highly for their works' sake. However, they are not to be our God.

When a leader crosses the line of responsibility and respect for God's people it leads to control. If we are controlled, we are not free to follow. If our freedom is lost and we still follow, we are in fear. Fear has no place in the lives of believers. God has not given us the spirit of fear.

Setting boundaries protects our personhood, our inner self, who we are, and who we are allowed to be in Christ. God wants us to live. In living, He wants us to fulfill our God-given purpose as we are thriving and abiding in Him. Amen!

CHAPTER 11

WARNING SIGNAL NO. 3: PROPAGATING THE SPIRIT OF FEAR

OW DO FALSE leaders deceive us and draw us into bondage? They use sophisticated techniques of brainwashing and mind control. One powerful tool is to instill fear in the unsuspecting follower. Fear of failing God, fear of dying and going to hell (eternal damnation), fear of displeasing the leaders—and the list goes on.

Since the heart of the believer does not want to fail God or displease their leaders, this proven tool of fear is used to keep you, the follower, subordinate and subservient (useful in an inferior capacity).

The fear of man is a strong force and one of the devil's most successful weapons. When it is used to exercise control over another person's life it is not a godly practice. "Fearing people is a dangerous trap, but trusting the LORD means safety" (Prov. 29:25, NLT). In another scripture it says, "It is better to trust in the Lord than to put confidence in man" (Ps. 118:8).

If you are a fearful person by nature, you are susceptible to almost any spirit of manipulation and control. This problem will exist in you until you yield to the power of the Holy Spirit, who will perfect peace and love inside of you.

Fear has torment. Your mind constantly feels guilty and has rushing thoughts running rampantly through it. First you concentrate on what you think the leaders are thinking about you and how you can make it better. Then you make up excuses to try to exonerate yourself from what you think they are thinking. It is a vicious cycle and leaves you confused, exhausted, and miserable. Fear brings on physical, mental, and emotional pain.

Being afraid of man is a horrible way to live your Christian life— or in any existence.

Biblical Warnings

The Book of Hebrews tells us that angels are sent to minister to those who are heirs of salvation (Heb. 1:14). How thankful we should be for this great truth, especially new Christians who enter the faith as infants. All believers need the protection of ministering angels. We all need a lot of tender loving care.

In his preparation to leave them, Paul the apostle sent for the elders of the church at Ephesus and rehearsed with them the past two years of work he had accomplished.

He then charged them to feed the flock of God (the sheep), over whom they were given authority, to nurture and to guard. His charge was directly given to the leaders and elders—also called overseers or bishops (Acts 20:17–28).

Now ready to depart their company, Paul gave a special warning. He tells them that grievous wolves (vicious wolves) would surely come in among them after he left. The false teachers would not care about those newly won to Christ. Paul also tells them that some of the elders currently in their presence would distort the truth to draw a following to themselves from the new disciples (Acts 20:29–28).

What an eye-opener! Here Paul mentioned corrupt leaders arising from those with whom he had spent at least two years, imparting truth and sharing doctrine on an apostolic level. Not only will they arise from among you, but some will even come in "shepherd's clothing." That is, they'll come in as loving, caring leaders. However, Paul declared they will be ravenous or grievous wolves.

Wolves mentioned in the Old and New Testaments from the Eastern lands of Syria and Palestine were the special enemy of the sheep and goats. Wolves were the dread of the shepherds. They symbolize treachery and cruelty. False teachers are likened to them.

Christ also warned in Matthew 7:15 that disciples should beware of false prophets who come to us in sheep's clothing, but inwardly are ravening wolves. In this scripture it means extortionists and robbers. They *pretend* to be sheep. Outwardly they often appear to be innocent, harmless, meek, useful, just, sanctified, devoted to God, and anointed by God.

But really they are the opposite: burdensome, violent, cruel, unsparing, fierce, spoilers, destroyers of the souls, out for dishonest gain, and just plain out to take advantage of you.

These warnings are found throughout the Word of God, both Old and New Testaments. Why then are Christians so vulnerable to false teachers? Do we ignore the warnings in the scripture because of fame and popularity? When did man's acceptance override God's Word?

Man's preference did not work when Israel insisted on having a king to rule over them like the other nations, rather than having the Lord. They got their wish. Saul was put on the throne as the first king of Israel. The downfall of his life was pride, egotism, and the abuse of power. This all led to his moral degradation and ruin. He was one of the bad leaders of Israel (1 Sam. 8–30).

Paul describes what a bad leader is for the church at Corinth. He said, "These people are false apostles. They have fooled you by disguising themselves as apostles of Christ. But I am not surprised! Even Satan can disguise himself as an angel of light. So it is no wonder his servants can also do it by pretending to be godly ministers. In the end they will get every bit of punishment their wicked deeds deserve" (2 Cor. 11:13–15, NLT).

Paul really loved the people and taught them in purity and in truth. The teacher, now leaving, could do nothing less than warn his students of the dangers that lie ahead. Since it is so easy for these false religious leaders to come in and deceive, he profoundly proclaimed, "My beloved, B-e-w-a-r-e!"

Fear Propagator #1: Accusers of the Brethren

By his actions it is evident that the old serpent, Satan, hated the presence of God, but still he was willing to appear before Him to accuse God's people.

In Revelation chapter 12, there are several descriptive definitions of Satan, our conquered enemy. In verse 10 he is called "the accuser of the brethren". He accused them before their God night and day, or continually. Satan brought indictments and accusations against many of God's servants including Abraham, Isaac, Jacob, Moses, David, Job, Joshua the high priest, Nehemiah the wall builder, and many other Old and New Testament saints.

Few victories are won without a fight. Christians must fight the good fight of faith. Here are but a few who fought faithfully and won.

Job

The Book of Job tells us how Job had the fight of his life. In the first chapter we find that Satan attacked his character, his children, and his material possessions. In chapter 2 Satan attacked his health.

When they heard the news about Job, three friends came for a visit: Eliphaz, Bildad, and Zophar. They came to mourn with him and comfort him because trouble had engulfed him and his household. Throughout the remainder of the book, instead of encouraging him they accused him day and night trying to make him admit that this trouble had come upon him because of his sin. His personal trouble was quite enough to weigh him down, but to have friends constantly badger and assail him, just added fuel to the fire of attack upon his life.

In their accusations they tried desperately to get him to reveal his secret sins and fears. They called him names and pointed the finger of guilt at him. "Folly and wickedness," they proclaimed, "Admit it!" Job sat in the seat of despondency. He was perplexed, but not guilty of the awful accusations lodged against him.

His friendly accusers proceeded to dictate to him how he should act, think, and feel. They declared that they had all the right answers, and that he should repent and listen to them. When Job did not confess and repent, they hurled fear and guilt on him because he did not do exactly as they had suggested.

There is nothing new under the sun. The same techniques used on Job, God's servant, can and will be used on you, God's servant. Heed this warning. If it has not already happened, it can. You could be ever so innocent, but they will come up with a list of faults and sins to lay blame on you. It is their intent to accuse you enough to make you feel sorry enough to repent and submit to them. With fancy words and innuendos they will twist what you say to mean what they want it to mean.

Nehemiah

Read the Book of Nehemiah. The Lord put a burden on this man to rebuild the walls of Jerusalem. Nehemiah had three enemies,

Sanballat, Tobiah, and Geshem, who formed a conspiracy against him. Their intentions were to entrap him and keep him from completing the work the Lord had assigned him to do.

Nehemiah's enemies purposely lied about him and sent letters to officials to stop his progress. They wanted him to stop the work of rebuilding the wall and come down to talk with them about their false accusations.

Sanballat told Nehemiah that a rumor had been started stating that Nehemiah and the Jews were rebelling. He said that Nehemiah wanted to be king, and that he had prophets prophesying in Jerusalem to that end (Neh. 6:6–8). Nehemiah recognized that these were just lies and rumors. In fact Nehemiah spoke back boldly to Sanballat and told him that he knew he was lying and that there was no truth in any part of his story. Nehemiah's remedy to his problem was to pray for strength to continue working, despite the opposition.

Intimidation is a great tool of accusers. They use it to break your spirit and to make you give up. You cannot chase a lie or false accusations. It is a waste of your time.

Throughout his task Nehemiah stayed in constant prayer and talked to the Lord about everything. He was focused and would not come down to the level of his accusers to discuss those lies.

When your enemies are accusing you, you too must be continuously in prayer. The Lord will talk to you and guide you every step of the way. You will know victory by your obedience to Him and by not yielding to the fear of man. Nehemiah knew their tricks and schemes but refused to yield. He had no fear of them because he trusted in his God.

You need not fear any spiritual leader. They have no control of either heaven nor hell. The scripture commands us to honor and respect the leaders. That involves understanding the call of God in their lives and the position and office of service to which God has called and placed them. We are always to respect authority, in the church and outside of the church. But we are never commanded to place them above God in authority over us.

The accusations that the enemy used against Nehemiah can also be used against you. The devil uses the same tricks. They work so well, why should he change? You may, therefore, be accused of being rebellious or wanting to be in authority over your leaders. They will say that you are trying to disrupt or destroy the organization. Don't believe their lies.

Stay humble before the Lord and stand fast in the liberty wherewith Christ has made you free (Gal. 5:1). If your heart is wholly submitted to the Lord you are, no doubt, the opposite of what you are being accused. Instead of rebellious, see yourself as God sees you: a strong solider, more than a conqueror. You are not a conqueror to overthrow an existing organization determined to be in error. You are a conqueror who walks in freedom and liberty in Christ.

Ask God to open your spiritual eyes so you can see yourself as one who is led by the Spirit of God. Visualize that you are a submissive vessel of honor, fit for the Master's use, leaning on the everlasting arms of Jesus.

Just as Nehemiah knew the truth about himself, you must know yourself. It's not that you want to be in authority over your leader or that you are calling people to follow you. These accusations are lies and the accuser knows it. He wants to convince you and others that it is the truth. He will shout it loud and clear and repeat it over and over again.

A person fighting for freedom from religious bondage does not want to be in charge himself. He has realized the awesomeness of being in the will of God and following the leading of the Holy Spirit. He understands that leaders are called, chosen, and appointed by almighty God. They must be sent. He knows that it is dangerous to go out on your own, so he wouldn't dare.

You may be crying out to God to search your heart, because you hear the accusations the enemy is loudly declaring. Learn to listen to the soft, sweet voice of the Holy Spirit as He gently tells you, "I know your heart. Trust me."

David and Saul: Jealousy comes between them

Jealousy is an ugly, evil force. Here are two definitions to consider:

1.   Being hostile toward a rival or one believed to enjoy an advantage

2.   Being intolerant of rivalry or unfaithfulness.

If you are looking for balance and liberty and have run into opposition because of it, an accusation you will most likely be confronted with is jealousy. Misguided leaders will attempt to silence you by accusing you of being jealous of a leader. They do not care if you are jealous of a regular member. Leadership is more important and accusing you of jealousy on that level gives the impression that it is a serious indictment. Don't believe their accusations against you.

A jealous person can cause discontentment and animosity. Jealousy breeds resentment and competition. Look around you; this is what you will see when jealousy is manifested.

Several other words and phrases closely related to jealousy are: covetous, demanding, grasping, grudging, envious, green-eyed, invidious (obnoxious and envious), mistrustful, suspicious, doubting, and questioning. Think about these words in relationship to a spirit of jealousy.

These words speak loud and clear. They do not describe you, do they? Prayerfully they would not.

You must take immediate steps to resist and eradicate from your mind the suggestion that you are jealous. If you don't do this, you will slowly begin to believe the lie. You will begin to say to yourself, "Well, maybe they are right. I do feel ill feelings toward this person sometimes." Cast down that imagination right now, in the name of Jesus!

In its worst state, jealousy can lead to murder. The example in Scripture often used is King Saul and David. We read of Saul's attempt to murder David on more than one occasion. Let's consider the reason why.

Saul was the first king of Israel. The Bible says, "Saul was the most handsome man in Israel—head and shoulders taller than anyone else in the land" (2 Sam. 9:2, NLT). He was a man anointed and filled with the Spirit, and in his early years he was humble and practiced self-control. Unfortunately, he did not remain that way. He became prideful, egotistic, disobedient, self-willed, and his abuse of power led to his moral degradation and ruin (1 Sam. 12–30).

David, on the other hand, was carefully chosen by God Himself as Israel's second king. He came from a low estate of tending his father's sheep, but God raised him up to sit upon the throne of Israel (1 Sam. 16). David was a courageous champion, proven to win many battles. First Samuel 18:5 tells us that David "behaved himself wisely" and "he was accepted in the sight of all the people, and also in the sight of Saul's servants."

Saul brought David into his home because he saw David as a mighty warrior, a favored man and an effective leader. But because of his *insecurity* and *fear*, Saul turned against David and began looking at him with suspicion. He knew that the Spirit of God was on David, but still proceeded to view him as his enemy. His ultimate plots against David led to his own defeat.

Who was jealous of whom? David was not jealous of Saul, but Saul was jealous of David. Yes, it was Saul the leader, the one in authority who was jealous of David. The people favored David for his warrior skills and sang a song of triumph exalting him over their existing king, Saul (1 Sam. 18:5–9). Saul's accusations against David were unfounded. He was motivated by his own jealousy and envy toward David. David was not the enemy as Saul thought he was. David respected Saul as Israel's King.

David had a chance to destroy Saul, but even though Saul was pursuing him, he chose to respect God's leader, and did not take his life. Although Saul was functioning in error and his life displeased God, he was still the leader.

Unfortunately, legalistic leaders attempt to eliminate those whom they view as threats to them or their agenda. If they cannot keep a person subservient, they will try to move them out. If they refuse to leave, they attempt to discredit them among the people who love them. This forces them to leave their organization because they no longer feel loved and accepted. Legalists may also excommunicate you, or just plain ask you to leave. More simply, they kick you out!

King Saul failed to realize that David did not anoint himself, his anointing came from God above. Many jealous leaders try to kill the anointing on a person's life. They really should complain to God and ask Him why He would put such an anointed, well favored person under their leadership. Instead they think that they are doing God's service by condemning and persecuting the person who has become a threat. They are bent on getting that person in line. Actually they know quite well that the problem is within them. However they will transfer the guilt just to keep from accepting the blame themselves. It's a fact.

Jesus

It was the religious leaders and others who lied about our Lord and Savior Jesus to make sure that He was falsely accused and punished. They challenged His doctrine every chance they could. But Jesus knew their thoughts and deceitfulness and continually outsmarted them. For this they hated Him, and that hatred grew worse day by day.

You can learn to answer false teachers wisely. Just listen to the Lord and follow His leading. They will not like you, and you can be sure that they will plot to ruin you and your reputation. But remember, Jesus "made himself of no reputation, and took upon him the form of a servant" (Phil. 2:7).

Jesus was arrested and brought before the council (Caiaphas the high priest, the scribes, and the elders); then before Pontius Pilate the governor, who found out that He was under Herod's jurisdiction, so he sent Him there. Everyone was talking about this prophet, Jesus. Curiosity was keen in both Pilate and Herod. Although Pilate and Herod did not like each other and were considered to be enemies, they came together as acquaintances so that they could be in one accord when the people began persecuting Jesus (Luke 22:66; 23:1–12).

You must remember this significant point: there are leaders who have been enemies for sometime that will put away their feuding and become comrades just to join a conspiracy against one of God's servants. To protect themselves from being exposed as wicked or evil, enemies will join forces against the righteous. We see this throughout the Scriptures. The aim of your enemy is to put you down by whatever means necessary before you reveal their motives and stop their selfish gains.

The chief priests, the scribes, and the crowd stood before Herod vehemently accusing Jesus. Such forceful accusations seemed so real, but they were as false as the leaders screaming them. Herod sent Jesus back to Pilate because he could not understand what the people saw in Jesus that was worthy of such persecution.

Pilate stood now again before the accusers who were bellowing out loud and boisterous words of condemnation. He tried to reason with them that neither he, nor Herod could find anything worthy of death that this Man had done (Luke 23:13–20). But Jesus' accusers cried out the more, "Crucify him, crucify him!" (Luke 23:21).

Pilate took water and washed his hands before the people and declared that he was innocent of the blood of this just Man. He finally saw that the accusers were envious of Jesus and wanted Him out of their way. He had done no crime worthy of death (Matt. 27:24).

During these proceedings Jesus did not attempt to defend Himself against His accusers (Matt. 27:13–14). You too must also know when to speak and when to be silent. The Lord will fight your battles for you. It is very hard to stay silent, especially when lies are being told on you and about you.

The truth, however, needs no defense.

Jesus knew His followers would encounter the same kind of trouble and persecution, because they chose to follow Him. He had these comforting words to say to them:

> Remember the word that I said unto you, The servant is not greater than his lord. If they have persecuted me, they will also persecute you.
>
> —JOHN 15:20

They will go to great lengths to accuse and condemn you when you refuse to fit into their mold. Do not find yourself going along, just to get along. Ask yourself these questions right now: Am I putting up with fear, confusion, and feelings of guilt? Am I being spiritually abused?

The same characteristics are prevalent in the church today. False accusations will be used by religious leaders who want to manipulate and control their followers. Whether you're in a leadership position or not, it is not a manifestation of the Holy Spirit that we should become accusers of our brothers and sisters in Christ. It is a ploy to divide and conquer and should not be a practice among true believers. The strategy of legalistic leaders doesn't often vary. The simple techniques they use to propagate a spirit of fear in their followers works so well on unsuspecting souls, there is no need to change. Heed these examples of the words they may use to instill fear. Being aware of these techniques can protect you spiritually.

Fear Propagator #2: Slanderous Words

Satan is using you to destroy the great work we are doing. He's using you to destroy our leader (or our church).

Not one of you would ever want it said that you are being used by Satan. Not for a minute. Whatever you were told to do to stop being used by Satan, you'd quickly do it. The intent is to bring fear into your mind and heart so that you can be controlled. Your speech (what you say) and your performance (what you do) is constantly measured with other more submissive members. The guilt dispensed can be very subtle, but when it is consistent it can smother you and choke the very life out of you. You cannot bear up alone against this kind of manipulation.

Slanderous words are sharp and pierce deep. They belittle and depreciate your value as a person. Even if it is true that you have done or said something wrong, it is not the end of the world. If you have sinned or missed the mark, you just need to confess your sin to the Lord. He is faithful and just and will forgive you and cleanse you of all sin and unrighteousness (1 John 1:9). It is not necessary for you to live a guilt-ridden life. Jesus shed His blood at Calvary so that you would no longer walk in condemnation (Rom. 8:1).

Don't fall for that slanderous statement that Satan is using you. He's really using them! Don't be afraid to open your eyes and see the truth. Cleanse your thoughts by reading the Word of God daily. Be transformed by the renewing of your mind. Allow the Lord to show you His good and perfect will. Amen.

Fear Propagator #3: Personal Rejection

You are not living up to your potential. You seem to have lost the vision. We may have to replace you and find someone else more capable.

What an esteem buster! Just think, at one time you were exactly what they needed. Now, it seems, you've lost whatever it was you had.

Maybe you pulled back a little in attendance because you realized that you needed to spend more time with your family. Perhaps you questioned one of your spiritual leaders in an open assembly (a real no-no). A number of actions on your part could have sparked the need for this propagation. Whatever the reason, on comes the rejection, guilt, and fear. The purpose: to control you.

You might find that now you must work harder to improve their opinion of you. You pull out the old performance treadmill and away you go, working and working and working. The work you do might include volunteering for the bus ministry, cleaning the church, or helping in the nursery. You began running errands and making yourself available for anything that needs to be done. Trying to win favor, you work until you are exhausted. But nothing will change their opinion of you unless you totally submit to their bad leadership, and allow their totalitarian ways to rule you.

Fear Propagator #4: Defeatism

You are headed toward failure. If you do not obey us your life will end up disastrous. Before you came to us you were on a path of total destruction. We saved you and got your life together. We are your only hope for success. You can't make it without us. If you leave us, you have left God.

This is a strong, blatant, and offensive statement. It seems impossible to accept the fact that any respected leader would utter such an accusation, such a threat; but it happens all the time. Who made them judges over your life, your successes, your failures? What gives them the right to decide your future? Are they God?

The child of God should not receive this threatening message in their heart. No matter how loud or forceful it sounds, it is not from God. With confidence, you can reject those words and return them to the wind.

When you actually realize what has been propagated against you and its effects, it should provoke righteous indignation. Your entire life can be affected by their damaging exploits. Do not fall for this trick. Become a God pleaser, not a man pleaser. This is just a rejection by man. Concentrate on the fact that you are accepted by the Lord.

A Few Side Effects of Fear

Fear is such a crippling experience. Some people fear the future or the past; some fear other people. There is fear of failure, fear of commitment, fear of damnation, fear of authority, etc. Whatever the focus, fear can stifle your existence.

Fear produces different reactions in different people. In some the heart pounds, the hands get sweaty, and the mouth gets dry. Others become nervous, sometimes just around certain people. Some have stomachaches, headaches, and body aches. Some cry, some become chronic complainers, some become bitter and hateful and mumble and grumble. A spirit of confusion comes to some people and others feel shame, guilt, loneliness, sadness—and the beat goes on.

Fear can stop you dead in your tracks. It can paralyze as well as cripple your progress. People have gone into clinical depression, chemical depression, and emotional and physical breakdowns because of fear. It is ugly. It is just like the devil to use this tool to keep you in bondage.

Barbara experiences fear

In Chapter 1 you were introduced to Barbara Springfield, one of the key leaders in her church fellowship. One of the strategies that overwhelmed Barbara was the propagation of the spirit of fear. She experienced an unusual sense of unrest in her spirit, which she now realizes originated from the obvious shift in the leadership's spiritual attitude and the manner in which they handled their followers.

It took Barbara a number of years of praying, talking to the Lord, seeking His face through Bible study, and dialoguing with other seasoned spiritual leaders to fully understand the strategy that was used to bring her into bondage.

At first Barbara noticed a change in the actions of the inner circle leaders. Unbalanced characteristics that were not Christ-like had surfaced and were predominant in their demeanor. She thought, "Where did this come from?"

Barbara did not want to judge her leaders and it was a little difficult for her to discern what was really going on, perhaps she was a little naïve. There she was a part of the leadership herself right in the midst of her peers, yet she felt so different than the others. Suddenly they displayed a hard-core, strict, and rigid attitude. It was as if she never really knew them. They had changed.

"Are we moving away from sound doctrine, from the love of God and love for His people?" she questioned herself. Barbara was a significant part of this fellowship and was greatly concerned. There always appeared to be a unity and oneness existing in their inner circle. Yet now she wondered why she was feeling quite distant from the others. She certainly did not want to be a stumbling block. That spirit of unity is so important in accomplishing God's work.

Barbara couldn't help it. She started showing visible signs of concern; it was no longer hidden. What happens on the inside of us will often show on the outside. Rather than express a real, genuine concern for her, the other leaders grew suspicious of her.

Barbara felt she no longer had a choice, she had to confess her concerns. Legalists require you to open up and talk about your thoughts and feelings. When you reveal your thoughts, it gives them further insight on how to deal with you. At this point Barbara still had no clue that she was engulfed in a damaging, legalistic organization.

It was an unfortunate experience, but Barbara did open her heart and share her concerns. It was the beginning of the end of her enjoyment of her Christian life at that particular church. A rough road lay ahead of her, for her life was about to be devastated by master legalistic leaders.

The suspicions of the leaders caused them to treat Barbara differently. Their hopes and plans were to draw her mind away from the concerns she had expressed, and to draw her back into their realm of control. Barbara did not know to what degree she was being controlled. They wanted no independent or free thinker who would shed light on their hidden agendas, agendas that were presented as God ideas, God agendas.

The leaders began their propagation of gaining back their control over Barbara's thought life. They insisted on telling her how to think. Although she did not consider herself a weak person, Barbara could feel the spirit of fear gripping her continually and she had no idea why, or the magnitude of what was actually happening to her. Hindsight now allows her to reveal her story.

Attacks against her character with the intention of silencing her, grew stronger and stronger. Exactly what did she experience? Maybe you experienced the same thing: crying—lots of crying, run-a-way thoughts, and nervousness, then feelings of gloom, doom, unworthiness, inadequacy, despair, trapped, etc.

Barbara was unfamiliar with consistent feelings of despair. Despair did not match her personality. She was a happy, joyful person. She continually blamed herself for the unexplainable thoughts running through her mind. It was quite some time before she even suspected that the Holy Spirit was trying to introduce a warning signal to her. Naïve? Yes, she was. The real question, though: was she serving God, or man? Barbara still did not have full revelation of her surroundings, so she continued to voice her concerns in the meetings, only to have them always met with rebuttals and counterattacks against her character. She endured a constant and dreadful bashing of her character.

Fear Propagator #5: Character Bashing

When you experience character bashing you have become a target of one of Satan's traditional attacks. It is definitely not a new thing. Legalists have completely opened themselves to be used by Satan in this regard. Don't be disturbed or alarmed. They always deny that they are legalistic. In their state of elitism, they can only see themselves as walking in holiness as God commanded. They believe that they are deeply committed and submitted to God alone. They cannot see their error, although they read and study the Word of God continually.

Bible study is their hallmark. No one can do it as well as they can. They are champions at it. Pride in this area causes them to bash the character of others who are not as holy and profound as they are.

If you do not readily cooperate with their legalistic schemes, you become the object of their attack. They attempt to draw you completely in or drive you completely out of their midst. You cannot continue to be a part of the group without total unquestioning commitment. The verbalizations of your doubts and the questioning of your leaders must stop.

To bash someone's character is to verbally, sometimes with violence, strike or smash their personhood. Some bashers are much smoother than others, they have the ability to bash you softly and quietly. Before you realize it, you're bashed!

The quiet and soft bashing can be subtle, but the damage is just as effective. In fact you may not even know that you've just been bashed until you feel the effects later. Then you feel violated. Sometimes you rehearse what you should have said back to them. Don't panic. You are still the winner, even though it doesn't feel like it at the moment.

Bashing involves the perpetrator saying the meanest thing they can think of about you and to you. They really know you are not what they are accusing you of, but it's a necessary plot to attack you with words that will hurt and stop you. They want you to think that these things are true of you. They shout it loud and clear. Words can kill and deeply wound the inner man. They strike out at your personhood. Fifty years can pass and, if you're not properly healed, you will still feel the effects of damaging words. Recovery from such an attack can be a very long process. In fact many people never fully recover, but live the rest of their lives angry and dysfunctional. Some of these wounded souls never return to attending church as we know it today.

Wives have been abused by cutting words of rejection from their husbands. Children try desperately to overcome the harsh words ungodly parents speak over them. Siblings have rivaled for years and have voiced wounding words to each other that cut deeply. Controlling leaders launch words that have greatly injured their followers. These attacks are sent forth from the realm of the evil one. They come to do major damage: to kill, steal and to destroy you.

You cannot fight such battles alone. It should be recognized as spiritual warfare, a conspiracy against the real you. The real motive behind the attack is to buffet God, because you strive to walk upright before Him. Remember Job's dilemma? God was delighted with His servant Job. He boasted of him and called him upright, a man of integrity. How would you like to have your heavenly Father speak highly of you? God knew Job's heart, and was pleased (Job 2:3). Maybe you please God, too.

If you are having this experience, you must stop and consider the fact that it may not be you who's in error; even if it feels like you're wrong, even if you are angry and feel that you're not showing love, even if you feel you're not forgiving.

You must remember and acknowledge that feelings are merely feelings. Emotions are very unreliable. Don't condemn yourself, and never make a life-changing decision based on your emotions alone. Do not concentrate on your sin. You are fighting for your life—your spiritual life. Your concentration must be on the Lord. Righteous indignation (anger), comes into play here. There is a time that you must exercise tough love by not allowing yourself to be controlled. This is probably the time.

In addition you are now in a spiritual walk, and there is now no condemnation to those who are walking after the Spirit, and not walking after the flesh. You are born again (Rom. 8:1).

Back to Barbara's Story

Barbara began entertaining thoughts of leaving her church fellowship because the pain she experienced from control, domination, character bashing, and much more, was just too hard to bear. She felt so alone and thought she had no one she could really confide in, especially no one in her local fellowship.

Although she was unaware at the time, she had isolated herself from most of her family and friends. The church had become the major focus of her entire life. This is not a good practice. The pain and hurt was very deep because of this sacrifice. The effects of isolation made her feel that she had no way out. At that time Barbara did not have the confident assurance that God was with her, even though He was. The Holy Spirit was there all the time warning her, preparing her, and directing her. She was unable to accurately discern her situation. Perhaps God is with you now, but you don't know it. I pray that He reveals Himself to you now, even as you read this book.

Barbara told of a dream she had during this difficult time. Actually the Lord dealt with her through several dreams. This particular dream involved what appeared to be an office building with a very long corridor. The hallway had lots of rooms with doors that were locked. Barbara sensed danger and tried to find her way out of the building through one of the doors, but none of them opened and she was trapped. As she rushed down the corridor she tried and tried, but could not open any of the doors. "There must have been at least a hundred doors," she said, but no way of escape was found.

Feeling trapped and closed in, Barbara awoke from this dream puzzled. Later, of course, she understood that the dream depicted her current situation; the closed in feeling, the isolation, the bondage, and the feeling of having no way out. These were just her feelings. God always has a way of escape. He is our way out.

Barbara continued trying desperately to fit in at church, but her conscience would not allow her to agree to all they were requiring. A totally exhausted Barbara finally confessed her desire to leave. The leaders' response was definite. "No one leaves our church, especially not one of our leaders. How would that look to outsiders? We have a reputation to uphold."

An unbelievable attack of fear was just about to overwhelm Barbara. In their final and desperate attempt to manipulate her, the leadership pulled out their super fear blaster. They said to her, "You will fail God if you leave us. What's the matter with you? The devil has gotten a hold of your mind."

What a lie from the pit of hell!

If you are in this situation now, help is on its way. It is imperative that you heed the warning signals of the Holy Spirit. They speak loud and clear throughout the Word of God. Let no one deceive you. Where the spirit of the Lord is, there is liberty: not pain; not despair; not damnation; not defeatism (2 Cor. 3:17). Once you're born again, you cannot be unborn. You have eternal security in Christ Jesus. No one can pluck you out of His hand!

The Holy Spirit is always available for you. He's ready and willing to go to work on your behalf. Thoughts of fear and the imaginations that come to torment you will be pulled down by God's mighty weapons and by His outstretched hand.

> (For the weapons of our warfare *are* not carnal, but mighty through God to the pulling down of strong holds;) Casting down imaginations, and every high thing that exalteth itself against the knowledge of God, and bringing into captivity every thought to the obedience of Christ.
>
> —2 CORINTHIANS 10:4–5

Barbara will overcome the fear that assails her. You too can know victory if you're willing to fight the good fight of faith and persevere through trials, persecution, and tribulations.

God's love, grace, and mercy will lead you into a powerful spirit of victory over the stronghold of fear.

Much of the trauma Barbara experienced was due to a continual attack of fear. She cried out to the Lord for help and He sent the answer through several avenues.

Read more of Barbara's story in Part II, Warning Signal No. 4, Chapter 12, The Transference of Guilt. Just when she thought it could not get any worse, the attacks against her multiplied.

The Balance

The fear of man bringeth a snare: but whoso putteth his trust in the Lord shall be safe.

—Proverbs 29:25

I, even I, am he that comforteth you: who art thou, that thou shouldest be afraid of a man that shall die, and of the son of man which shall be made as grass.

—Isaiah 51:12

The fear of man is a dangerous trap. When wicked men know that you are afraid of them, you become tools to fulfill their wickedness. The Lord reminds us that it is He who encourages us, and that we should never fear mere humans because they will dry up and wither away, just like grass.

No matter what position of authority a spiritual leader holds, he is not greater than our God, and the Lord is not pleased when a Christian leader intimidates one of His beloved.

Abraham trapped by fear

For the believer, fearing man can cause a boomerang effect in his or her life. It can bring up temptations and cause actions that may backfire. For instance, in Genesis chapter 20 it tells a story of when Abraham went to Gerar and found himself in unfamiliar territory among unfamiliar people. Have you ever been somewhere for the first time and were afraid of your surroundings? Let's not judge Abraham too quickly and too harshly.

Abraham was afraid that he might be killed and the people would take his beautiful wife Sarah from him. Fearing man and fearing for his life, Abraham lied and told the people in Gerar that Sarah was his sister. King Abimelech, therefore, immediately had Sarah brought in to him. He desired her because of her beauty. And, after all, Abraham said that he was her brother.

God intervened in Abraham's behalf. Abraham explained that what he said was a half-truth. Sarah was the daughter of his father, but not the daughter of his mother, and she became his wife. It was really a lie and had the potential of causing a great deal of trouble for a lot of people. To save the day God gave Abimelech a dream. In that dream God revealed that Sarah was Abraham's wife and God instructed Abimelech not to touch her.

God goes to work for his children even in the midst of their error and fears. So do not worry, child of God, He is on your side in spite of your fears. His will for us is that we do not fear man, but rather trust only in Him.

Peter trapped by fear

Peter also lied when his life was threatened, and three times denied knowing the Savior. It's easy to point the finger at these two, Abraham and Peter, whose fear of man had similar, but different consequences.

Under what circumstances can you too be found fearing man or fearing authority?

Reverence for God

The fear of the Lord is the beginning of wisdom.
—PSALM 111:10

We can know for sure that God wants His people to fear and reverence Him alone. Reverence for God is a distinctively different kind of fear, one to which we will gladly comply.

God's desire is that we walk in love and power, and that we thrive with a sound mind. Timothy, Paul's spiritual son, may have been prone to fear. It certainly is a fearful task leading God's people. But Timothy was admonished by Paul not to be overwhelmed by this spirit (2 Tim. 1:7). The gift of the Holy Spirit within us can be stirred up so that we can go forth leading God's people in the power of the Lord, not timidity.

Fear dissipates in the presence of our loving God. We must build a solid and sound relationship with Him. When our dependency is wrapped in Him, He will build our trust and confidence to a new level.

Leaders should not use fear and manipulation to get their followers to work and serve. A good leader leads by example.

Although great challenges lie ahead of Christians, God has commanded all of us not to be afraid, leaders and followers alike. He is Emmanuel, God with us (Matt. 1:23).

Leaders are subject to the Lord. If they are called by Him, He will deal with their folly in His own time. We should not fight against our leaders. Everyone is subject to Him (Psalm 75:7). Nebuchadnezzar, king of Babylon reigned for forty-three years and found out the hard way who ruled the universe. This king was a bold and proud ruler who exalted himself, only to be humbled by the hand of almighty God (Dan. 1–4).

Try the spirit, by the Spirit to see if it be of God (1 John 4:1). Be careful to whom you yield and how much of yourself you yield.

What a wonderful life of liberty and freedom we can know while abiding in Christ, as He abides in us!

Hear Our Prayer, Lord

Father, hear our cry. Lead us not into the temptation to fear man. Hold us in the depths of Your love. Guide us in the paths of righteousness. May we have confidence in You and be found pleasing in Your sight. Amen!

CHAPTER 12

WARNING SIGNAL NO. 4: THE TRANSFERENCE OF GUILT

O NE EXAMPLE OF guilt being transferred from one's self to another is recorded in the third chapter of Genesis. The Garden of Eden is where sin entered the world, and the vehicle through which sin gained its access is mankind. Eve ate the forbidden fruit first, then gave it to Adam. The Bible says Eve was deceived, but Adam ate willingly. Sin with all of its consequences had penetrated God's creation through this one act of disobedience.

Before we see the transference of guilt, we find God and Adam engaging in a question and answer conversation. God confronts Adam and asks him three important questions.

The first question God asks is, "Adam, where are you?" Adam answered and stated four things: I heard your voice, I was afraid, I was naked, and I hid myself (Gen. 3:9–10).

Although this is not a commentary on the fall of mankind, it is necessary for us to understand the awfulness of guilt and why people would prefer to pass it on to someone else.

Upon eating from the forbidden tree of the knowledge of good and evil, Adam and Eve were arrested by sin and died spiritually. Shame and fear were immediately manifested. Shame is the painful emotion caused by a consciousness of guilt. In other words, the eyes of their consciousness were opened, and they were now aware of the disorder inside of them. This was not an ordinary disorder but one of great magnitude. They were not aware of this consciousness before they disobeyed God.

Under this new awareness, they both realized that they were naked. Were they not naked before? Yes. Why now at this point were they ashamed? Something more has entered the atmosphere: fear. Previously, they knew no shame, no dread, no fear. Fear expressed itself with dread and shame. Adam and Eve heard the voice of God and were terrified because they were naked. They hid from the presence of God. Heretofore, it was a pleasure to be in God's presence, not dread, not terror (Gen. 3:7–8).

Adam said, "I was afraid." With fear also comes an evasive and cowardly spirit. Adam wanted to run and hide himself because he had lost his first estate, and he knew it. Yes, he lost a blessed estate. One of dignity—now lost, and grace—now disgrace. Adam was degraded, disarmed, and disrobed of honor. This act of disobedience was much deeper than we care to admit. The peace that Adam and Eve once knew was gone.

They thought their eyes would be opened, and so they were, but it did not yield the pleasure they anticipated. Instead, their eyes were opened to their shame and grief. They were not opened in a favorable way; nor was it as gratifying as the serpent proposed (Gen. 3:4–5).

Their natures were corrupted, they found themselves hiding from their loving Creator God. The picture is painted here of someone who is feeling pretty lousy inside—in his mind. It is a painful spot to be in. Everything Adam said in answer to God's first question points to how horrible he felt. Notice how many times he used the word "I." Reading from the King James Version we count four times and once he added *myself*. He said, "I hid myself" (Gen. 3:10). Adam is now very conscious of himself.

Legalism will cause people to be unduly self-conscious—conscious of how things will affect them; conscious of what might be taken from them or added to them; conscious of what might be said about them. They are constantly examining and measuring themselves and their surroundings.

The pain associated with guilt is not what they want to experience. They will avoid it at all costs. Life for a legalist revolves around himself. He is always the center of attention and greatness. Therefore he will transfer guilt to the innocent, to the unsuspecting follower, to anyone who will accept that guilt. This appeases his own conscience, even if only for a short period. The legalist must exalt himself and give himself accolades. In addition he must be embraced and receive accolades from those who serve under his leadership.

The member who is caught up in following a legalistic leader is most likely unaware why he himself is self-conscious. He's continually made to feel insufficient, so he measures what he does and says by what his leader thinks of him. Since the leader keeps him subordinate, he's always going to be self-conscious, and he'll always try to please his leaders.

Back to Adam

The creator God asked the created man, "Where art thou?" (Gen. 3:9). The response from the created one was a response of fear, shame, and guilt. Of course we know that when God asks a question, He already knows the answer. God knew exactly where Adam was physically and spiritually, but the question was asked so that Adam might be made aware.

Since we know that God was not interested in Adam's physical location, but rather his eternal condition, what exactly was He asking Adam? Where are you? In essence, have you moved away from Me, away from our covenant, our relationship? Did you prefer another over me? Have you lost your innocence? The question is intended to humble a fallen man who had yielded to the lust of his flesh, the lust of his eyes, and the pride of life.

If you are a leader, where are you? Have you lost a certain degree of your innocence because you have continually disobeyed God? Are your desires perverted, out of whack? I know you started out very humble and submissive to the Father, but over the months and years, has your busy-ness and your work for the Lord kept you from spending time with the Lord of the work?

The Transfer

Now the attempt to transfer the guilt. Consider his paraphrased response. Adam said, "It's really not my fault." Then whose fault is it? The first name Adam gave to transfer blame was the "woman." The second name Adam gave was the woman "You" gave me. So in essence Adam attempted to transfer the guilt to Eve and even to God. The guilt was so painful, the fear was so great, and the shame was so convicting that Adam had to get it off of him and on to someone else. Why not send the blame back to the giver (Gen. 3:12)?

How many of us are blaming God for our circumstances or for the outcome of a past event in our lives. If we transfer that responsibility to someone else, we won't have to bear it ourselves, right?

Guilty leaders will often try to transfer feelings of guilt to their members. If they can keep their members feeling guilty, no sin, error, or fault can revert back to them. It's a tricky maneuver. Let this be a warning signal for you.

It's as if Adam thought God would agree with him and take the blame, by saying, "You're right, I guess I made a mistake." Was not our Creator God omniscient? Was Adam suggesting that God didn't know everything, past, present, and future? Could Adam convince God that it was *His* fault? I can hear Adam now, making his argument. "God, if you had never given me this woman, I would never have eaten." He essentially made God a co-conspirator with Eve. They both caused him to disobey. That sounds foolish, right? Yet we do it ourselves many times.

Do you control others to get the job done? It is so easy to be beguiled by Satan when we are over worked and overwhelmed.

Perhaps you are not a leader, but maybe you're being wooed by a leader who's not fully operating under God's wonderful grace. Is there someone desiring to have rule over you? Do you feel guilt being handed to you continually? Do not allow another to take the place of God in your life. Let God be God.

When we move toward putting another person, an organization, or anything in God's place as deity or Lord over us, we have moved away from Him. This is what Adam and Eve did when they obeyed the serpent and disobeyed God. Our heavenly Father might ask us that same question that He asked Adam, "Where art thou?" (Gen. 3:9). Have you moved out of the will of God by allowing another to control you? Are you the controller or the controlled?

Paul asked a similar question to the Christians at Galatia, "Who hath bewitched you, that ye should not obey the truth...?" (Gal. 3:1). Many of God's beloved have believed the lies of false teachers who desire to rule over them and entangle them in bondage.

The Second and Third Questions
Also Introduce Adam's Attempt to Transfer Guilt

> Who told thee that thou *wast* naked? Hast thou eaten of the tree, whereof I commanded thee that thou shouldest not eat?
>
> —GENESIS 3:11

Still dealing with the man, a confession is sought. He wants to know how it is that Adam is aware of his nakedness.

Instead of owning up to his sin, Adam's pain was so great that he could not handle it. The sting of guilt and fear is so great that you probably can't handle it either. You need a Savior to bear it for you. That's exactly what our Lord Jesus did. He bore our sin on the cross, once and for all.

Guilt and condemnation are so different from conviction. The Holy Spirit will convict and convince us of sin and all unrighteousness that we might repent and come back in line with His commandments. Yes, we will feel really bad, but not hopeless. Fear, guilt, and condemnation make you feel utterly hopeless. They make you feel that God no longer loves you, that you are not worthy to be called His child.

Conviction will not deliver this result. If you experience conviction you feel compelled to tell the truth. Someone on the inside (the Holy Spirit) will strongly persuade and convince you that it is to your best interest to admit your sin or error, and get right with God. When you're cleansed, you feel relieved, you feel wonderful. You feel God has forgiven you and you are free. Oh what a difference the truth makes in your life!

Whatever happened to this kind of conviction in the life of believers today? Have we lost it? If so, how do we get it back?

The legalistic leader will cause you to think that you are the guilty one by transferring guilt to you. You might even feel you are wrong, but you could be right. When you are encountering matters with them, don't fret. Hold on until God speaks.

But even if you are wrong—and sometimes you will be—it's not the end of the world, as they will make you feel. The fact is when they sin or err, you seldom hear them confess any wrongdoing. Like Adam and Eve, they aren't often able to handle facing their wrong. It is very painful.

Your personal consolation is that one day the false teachers and leaders will stand before a righteous God and give an account for the wrong they have done. Do not try to prove them wrong. They will not hear you. Make your statements, say what you need to say, and move on. Legalists like to keep you in a discussion with them for hours. Do not subject yourself to an unlimited time with them. They would love to wear you down and wear you out with a long deliberation. Remember when you move on do not, I repeat, do not take any guilt with you. Do not agree with them that you are guilty. Do not try to figure out where you went wrong, maybe you didn't. If you did, the Holy Spirit will convict you, not condemn you.

The transference of guilt is ever so smooth. Before you know it everything is on you and off the perpetrators. Do not be taken in by this tactic. Adam's attempt to transfer the guilt to the woman and to God did not work. You must not let it work with you either.

Back to Robert's Story

In Chapter 1 we introduced Robert Winters, a member of the Tabernacle Church. He was plagued with doctrinal differences, with fear, and with guilt about simple Christian living. His leaders volleyed Bible doctrine so much that it was hard for him to find stability in their teachings. He was very inquisitive about the Word of God and was the type who asked a lot of questions. Unfortunately his leaders were not the type who believed that a member should question the leadership. As a result he was deemed to be a troublemaker, and one who sowed discord among other members. He was also labeled as one whose every step needed to be watched.

Robert felt the leaders had challenged his manhood before the other members on a continual basis. He also felt he had lost the respect of many members because of it. He was verbally put down, and many of his legitimate questions were met with public ridicule. No one wants to be the brunt of such intimidation.

Feeling dejected and having very little peace inside, Robert sought godly counsel outside of the Tabernacle. Sometimes you must step out of the box long enough to see what could possibly be wrong inside of the box. When you examine the contents of a box from the outside looking in, you often get a better perspective of what's really in there.

Robert's godly counselors were God sent. They included men and women of God who had the ability to offer him the wisdom he needed to get through his pain. They walked him through a systematic theology of Christian doctrine that soon began to alleviate his confusion. In this process Robert revealed some deep-seated opinions he had, which were the result of years of verbal abuse from Christian leadership. He was wounded and full of anger. "Christianity was not supposed to be like this," he thought.

It took months of Bible study to unravel basic Christian doctrine, and to pull the scales off Robert's eyes. As his counselors taught him the Word of God, Robert put his trust in the Holy Spirit's ability to reveal truth to him. The other teachers had greatly confused him.

God's Grace Is Revealed to Robert

And of His fulness have all we received, and grace for grace. For the law was given by Moses, but grace and truth came by Jesus Christ.

—JOHN 1:16–17

Several months into his new teaching sessions, Robert received a revelation about God's grace. Learning the Word of God was not as hard as he had thought. When presented from a legalistic standpoint, Bible teaching brings us into bondage, not freedom or grace. Robert had tried to understand what his teachers were teaching, but he would always end up questioning them over and over again. Most of what they taught did not make sense. He had tried ever so hard to live up to what they taught, but was consistently frustrated.

Robert discovered that the teachers were trying to get him to follow a set of rules. He could never keep those rules or measure up to what his teachers said he should do. He felt like a failure all the time. He spent many nights repenting and feeling like a rebel because he could not live up to all the do's and don'ts. That's where his anger originated. That's where the questions came from. He felt if he had the answers to his questions, he could start obeying what they said. It was futile, a vicious circle.

It was legalism, and with legalism you never measure up, you never catch up, and you're always working to be accepted. You always feel like you're not good enough. Following a set of man-made rules does not get us to heaven, does not get us saved, does not make us accepted in the sight of God. Accepting Jesus Christ as our Savior is the only way. He paid the price for us at Calvary.

The Gospel of John teaches that the Law of Moses had its place in revealing man's condition and his need of God. It is God's grace that pardon's our sins. Grace and truth came to us through Jesus Christ. Robert needed only to understand and accept grace. The Lord has given us a new covenant, a covenant of grace. The letter of the law brings death, but the Spirit brings life.

These revelations helped Robert tremendously. He also learned that whenever he questioned his leaders at the Tabernacle, it provoked them to transfer guilt to him. They did not want to be questioned; they did not want to be wrong in any way. The pain was unbearable so they refused it by pushing it off onto Robert. He missed that warning signal over and over again and suffered a long time at their hands. Robert was a simple believer. He tried and tried to understand, to see it their way. It never happened. It was very frustrating.

Once Robert received a revelation of grace he was on his way to recovery from legalism. Read the conclusion of his story in Part III, Chapter 15, Look and Live.

Back to the Garden of Eden: Adam and Eve

Adam's attempt to transfer the guilt from his disobedience to Eve and to God did not work. However, God dealt with the two sinners quite differently than you or I would have, I'm sure. We do not have His perfect grace, His perfect love, or His everlasting mercy. God certainly did not debate the issues with Adam and Eve. Agape (God's unconditional love) stepped in, manifested its awesomeness, and prevailed.

There were consequences, of course, for the man, the woman, and the serpent. The entire creation was affected by this one act of disobedience. Although we often discuss the temptation and the fall, it was the magnificent love the Father has for us all that boggles my mind. He would not leave us in this separated state. He understood that man would disobey Him, but still loved us enough to create us and make provision to continue a wonderful fellowship with us. Redemption's provision is revealed before Genesis chapter 3 is concluded.

More Trouble for Barbara: Transference of Someone Else's Guilt to Her

In Chapter 11, we left Barbara in quite a predicament. She had suffered greatly under a spirit of fear, character bashing, and now guilt was added. There was not much that Barbara did or said among her leaders that was treated with respect. "Why be a part of the leadership if I'm resented," she thought.

In the leaders' meetings Barbara's ideas were continually shot down and met with defeat. After being pressed to talk and offer suggestions, Barbara's sincerity was scorned. Nearly every thought she expressed was met with disdain. She seemed to do nothing right in their sight. Whatever she said was twisted, turned, and used against her. Time and time again they hurled guilt upon her for any and everything. She could not believe what was happening.

She left most of these business meetings broken, crying, and shattered. "This cannot be the spirit of God," she thought.

Some leaders' ability to transfer guilt to another person is uncanny. It is their intention never to be wrong in the sight of their followers. They function as the world's greatest prosecuting attorneys when it comes to shifting the blame and creating evidence to use against you. They can also instantly change, transform their tactics, transform their conversation, and become the world's greatest defense attorney when it comes to defending and exonerating themselves. They prosecute you; they defend themselves. It's the truth.

Barbara fought through tears, heartache, slander, rejection, and anger. She grew tired and weary—physically and emotionally exhausted.

Unable to communicate effectively with them and having no other recourse, she ran fast to the throne of grace. What a wonderful place to go!

At the throne of grace, the Holy Spirit took the blinders off her eyes, once and for all. The Lord began to pour understanding into her heart. She realized that she was in a spiritual battle, a war which had already been won by Christ.

Absolute Victory for Barbara!

Like so many others, Barbara had come face-to-face with the ugly spirit of legalism. It attempted to crush and to break her. Its goal was to bring her into submission and subjection to its rule over her life. That's bondage. That's what this spirit desires of you—to keep you bound, confused, and submissive to man, not to our loving heavenly Father. A submissive spirit is a desirable attribute, but not to the point that the submissive one is manipulated and controlled. That's not what the scripture means when it asks us to submit one to another.

It was the eighth chapter of Romans that brought great revelation to Barbara as she meditated on the Word. The first verse brought reassurance to her concerning guilt and condemnation.

> There is therefore now no condemnation to them which are in Christ Jesus, who walk not after the flesh, but after the Spirit.
>
> —ROMANS 8:1

An illumination in Barbara's spirit lifted those evil spirits off of her by the power of the Holy Ghost. Barbara understood as never before that the guilt and penalty of sin had been removed at the cross. Nothing anyone would say to her should cause her to receive guilt or condemnation. If she should sin, Christ is her advocate with the Father: "And he is the propitiation [the sacrifice] for our sins: and not for ours only, but also for the sins of the whole world" (1 John 2:2).

The bondage holding Barbara began to dwindle fast as God revealed His Word to her. Day by day strongholds were exposed and broken. Verse by verse, the eighth chapter of Romans enlightened her on her position in Christ and His love for her. Guilt could no longer cause her to feel separated from His love.

Barbara sincerely appreciated the Lord. Although she had foolishly submitted on the wrong level to men, she really loved the Lord and had longed for a deep, intimate relationship with Him.

Please make sure that your relationship with the Father through His Son Jesus is intact. It is very important that you keep this intimate relationship throughout your process of getting free.

As she pondered all that had transpired, it was evident that she had grown to another level in her walk of faith. Legalism was exposed, the bondage of guilt was completely stripped away, and another level of God's grace was revealed. Her love for the Lord deepened. Today she is serving the Lord in this liberty and freedom at a new, balanced church fellowship—completely satisfied in Christ.

One final word needs to be said concerning Barbara's deliverance from legalism. Read her last step of victory in Part III, Chapter 13, A Desire to Be Free.

Love: the Balance and Antidote for Guilt

Who shall lay any thing to the charge of God's elect? It is God that justifieth. Who is he that condemneth? It is Christ that died, yea rather, that is risen again, who is even at the right hand of God, who also maketh intercession for us. Who shall separate us from the love of Christ? shall tribulation, or distress, or persecution, or famine, or nakedness, or peril, or sword? As it is written, For thy sake we are killed all the day long; we are accounted as sheep for the slaughter. Nay, in all these things we are more than conquerors through him that loved us. For I am persuaded, that neither death, nor life, nor angels, nor principalities, nor powers, nor things present, nor things to come, Nor height, nor depth, nor any other creature, shall be able to separate us from the love of God, which is in Christ Jesus our Lord.

—ROMANS 8:33–39

Part III

THE WAY OUT: TRANSITION AND RESTORATION

A SCRIPTURAL FOUNDATION

CHAPTER 13

A DESIRE TO BE FREE

B Y NOW MANY readers who are in legalism will be asking themselves, "How could this happen to me? Why did I allow myself to be manipulated and controlled?"

Some of you might be experiencing shame. Feeling shame is just part of the aftermath. It will pass if you understand its origin and then deny its absolute ownership over you. Shame is a real feeling, so you must refuse to let it reign in your mind.

Do not continue to live under the unpleasant influence of legalism? During your involvement you probably experienced many problems and failures, and you certainly had great challenges. But now you must realize that your Christian life experiences can change for the better.

Do not allow your past to hinder or dictate the progress, success, and advancement of your future. You must have a strong, vibrant desire to be free.

One of the most positive attitudes needed to achieve success in any endeavor is *desire*. You must want to be free—to be liberated, to be successful. Your family, friends, loved ones, and even Jesus wants you to be free. Desire is a strong action word. It means that you long for freedom, that you really want to walk in liberty in Christ. Desire stresses the strength of feeling. You must pursue freedom, run after it with all your might. It's attainable. You can have it. It waits for you to possess it.

The first chapter in Proverbs records wisdom's warning against the enticement of sinners. This passage of Scripture should reassure you that you do not need to be afraid of falling prey again to the wiles and schemes of legalistic pursuers (sinners) (Prov. 1:10–19). We only need to govern ourselves according to the warnings throughout the Word of God, and we shall be saved from their ensnarement.

When we sincerely study the Bible, and appropriately apply its precepts and principles to our lives, we will clearly and distinctly learn how to recognize false teachers. It is important for believers to sharpen their spiritual antennas. We must learn to discern between truth and falsehood, good and evil. As we learn to discern the difference, we will be better able to guard ourselves against anything that would try to draw us away from that truth.

Contrary to popular belief, the Bible is not hard to comprehend and follow. There are many simplified versions available written in today's language to help us understand what God is saying to His people. Proverbs teaches that even the simple, unlearned new believer can benefit by studying and obeying the Word of God.

> These are the proverbs of Solomon, David's son, king of Israel. The purpose of these proverbs is to teach people wisdom and discipline, to help them understand wise sayings. Through these proverbs, people will receive instruction in discipline, good conduct, and doing what is right, just, and fair. These proverbs will make the simpleminded clever. They will give knowledge and purpose to young people. Let those who are wise listen to these proverbs and become even wiser. And let those who understand receive guidance by exploring the depth of meaning in these proverbs, parables, wise sayings, and riddles. Fear of the LORD is the beginning of knowledge. Only fools despise wisdom and discipline. Listen, my child, to what your father teaches you. Don't neglect your mother's teaching. What you learn from them will crown you with

grace and clothe you with honor. My child, if sinners entice you, turn your back on them!

—PROVERBS 1:1–10, NLT

Proverbs is the book of wisdom. Even for those who really consider themselves to be an ordinary person of ordinary intelligence, Proverbs promises that they can learn to be smart. By the way, you are not just an ordinary person, you are God's beloved and you are very precious in His sight.

Receiving and applying the Word of God is your road map to the liberty and freedom in Christ that you seek. Become a doer of the Word, not just a reader or a hearer only. Desire change and you will be rewarded with change.

The real people introduced to you earlier—Susan, Barbara, Robert, and Curtis—were ready for change. Are *you* ready, my friend?

Conclusion of Barbara's Story: A Final Note of Victory

In Chapter 12 we indicated that Barbara had one last step to absolute victory. Heavy laden with fear, she had been through quite an ordeal at her legalistic assembly. She was afraid to leave and afraid to stay. If she stayed she would endure more character bashing, belittling, fear, and guilt. If she left, she had been told that she would be a failure and displease God.

We also learned that Barbara found victory through fasting, prayer, and by studying the Word of God. The trauma in her life diminished as she received a revelation of God's grace. Time will not allow me to elaborate on Barbara's entire story and her successful escape from legalism. But her safeguard was to stay *in* Christ. After her deliverance from legalism, Barbara knew she had to continue in the faith to effect the process of complete healing and restoration.

It was quite a spiritual battle that Barbara had come through, and she had learned a great deal about trusting God. Some people lose many battles trying to fight in their own strength, in their flesh. Successful spiritual battles, however, are won on your knees, in that secret place of the Most High.

She read 2 Corinthians 10:3–5 again, but this time from the New Living Translation. "We are human, but we don't wage war with human plans and methods. We use God's mighty weapons, not mere worldly weapons, to knock down the Devil's strongholds. With these weapons we break down every proud argument that keeps people from knowing God. With these weapons we conquer their rebellious ideas, and we teach them to obey Christ."

Occasionally Barbara looks back over the years she spent in bondage. But today a smile comes up in her spirit, instead of regret. She's thankful that the Lord heard her cry, and brought her out of a horrible pit. The pain she endured back then cannot compare to the joy with which she serves the Lord today. You see, she appropriated the Lord's healing balm and was set absolutely free, and whom the Son sets free is free indeed!

Forgiveness

Forgiveness was a vital key to Barbara's deliverance. She admits that it was not an easy thing to do, to forgive. She fought hard and long. The temptation to hold a grudge was keen. It is a powerful stronghold. If you want to live free, however, you must forgive. Don't try to do it alone. The Holy Spirit will help you to let go of the past.

A Taste of Freedom

There is a wonderful sigh of relief that Barbara experiences now that she is free. Once you have tasted real freedom and liberty in

Christ, you will never want to go back to bondage. In fact, you will spot the danger and warning signals miles away.

This last section of the book will be used to offer guidelines for your transition out of bondage and the way back to enjoying the Christian lifestyle, the abundant life that Christ intended.

The joy you will experience is unbelievable. Trust God. He will lead you every step of the way out of bondage, and every step of the way into His loving arms of freedom.

> O taste and see that the Lord is good: blessed is the man that trusteth in him.
> —PSALM 34:8

Although the road to freedom may feel lonely sometimes, you are never alone. You must continue to trust the Lord. Don't quit and don't give up. There are many people who identify with what you have gone through. Many have success stories and are willing to share them with you. Check the suggested resources in the back of this book.

A Legalism Reminder

Let's take another look at what legalism really is. Your desire to be free must supersede your willingness to stay in legalistic bondage.

In Chapter 7 we defined legalism straight from *Webster's Dictionary* as strict, literal, or excessive conformity to the law or to a religious or moral code, often which restricts free choice.

Now that you've read some real live examples, let's go a little further in our definition. Legalism is any system, rules, expectations, or regulations that promise God's love in return for human effort and obedience. It offers salvation as a reward for your performance.

We said legalism is much like a cancer because we respond to it much like our bodies respond to cancer. Cancer can be detected in one part of our body, then lead a path of destruction that runs rapidly throughout our entire body, contaminating every organ in its path. It eats away internally, then takes your life; you die physically.

Legalism will also eat away inside until the very life is taken out of you; your mind, your will, your emotions, and also your spiritual life. Legalism is a killer.

Treatment for cancer varies and may largely depend upon the stage of development when it is discovered. Side effects from treatments can also vary. Physicians and technicians have treated individuals with many different methods, from diet changes to chemotherapy, radiation, etc.

Legalism is like a spiritual toxic virus spread by religion. It is man's rules used to get to God. But unlike the diverse treatments for cancer, legalism is best treated by one significant thing: accepting God's marvelous, unconditional love, and bathing in His amazing grace.

So, my friend, set your desire, your passion, your affection, and your longing, on things that are above where Christ is seated on the right hand of God. With all your heart, desire that freedom in Christ. Remember, you are dead, and your life is now hid with Christ in God. Christ is now your life, and when He shall appear, then shall we also appear with Him in glory (Col. 3:1–4)!

Let's turn our attention now to some of the hindrances to getting free from legalism. We'll discuss what you are feeling and offer some suggestions as to why you're feeling that way. Then we'll share some important scriptural keys.

CHAPTER 14

SOUL TIES AND FANTASY BONDING

(THE PATHWAY TO BONDAGE)

RELATIONSHIPS FOUNDED ON sound Christian principles have the greatest potential to flourish (to thrive, to grow luxuriantly) or to be fruitful. That includes relationships between individuals and relationships between an organization and its members or associates. Many such relationships start out right, but it is crucial that each one continues to be supported and sustained by godly wholesome principles. Look at this example.

Welcome to Fantasy Land

A shy and naïve young girl left the security of her mother and father's home to marry her sweetheart. The two had dated for one year and she was sure that he was the right one. How surprised she was to learn that the wonderful relationship she enjoyed during their courtship was turned upside down when her new husband revealed another side of his character. Likewise, he was a little upset to learn that she was not all that he had originally anticipated.

During the courtship both were on their best behavior. They were in that enchanted stage of the relationship. Each was infatuated with the other one and both walked on cloud nine most of the time they dated. Neither of them ever really displayed the real truth about themselves. Both were too insecure to show their real faults, failures, errors, or weaknesses.

The young lady was always at her prettiest and the young man was always ever so handsome. No bad breath, shabby clothes, or tattered disposition was ever displayed between them. That describes their outward appearance, but does not nearly identify or touch their inward struggles. Yes they did have disagreements, but both gave a little and took a little and, in so doing, created a false interpretation of their real, unresolved issues. Inside character traits were not fully developed, so the pressure and struggles after the marriage ceremony stemmed from selfishness and other personal weaknesses.

In all their effort to live together trying to merge habits, personal desires, and lifestyles, they awoke one morning to find themselves in a predicament. Nothing was really real and the effort it takes to be who you really "are not" was too much for either of them to continue pretending. The real persons emerged and they didn't like what they saw in each other, so they entered a disenchanted stage of their relationship.

It seemed the devil was standing there all the time chanting, "Welcome to fantasy land." She was upset most of the time and he was also very uncomfortable and unhappy. They both felt they had made a terrible mistake by getting married. Both seriously wondered if they could even make it as husband and wife.

They agreed that they should see a marriage counselor. The sympathetic marriage counselor had some encouraging words for them. He said, "Hang in there folks, you're only at the beginning stage of your relationship. Marriage requires you to learn about each other and grow together. The process will continue to bring you closer together. Stage three is called maturity; you'll get there, eventually." To the unhappy couple maturity seemed a long way off, if attainable at all. They wanted immediate relief. The pain was too uncomfortable. Marriage was not supposed to be this hard, they thought.

The shy young girl who once thought "he's the one," rethinks the relationship and wonders now if their attraction to each other was only a fantasy, something that was never real. Was it founded on good solid principles such as truth and honesty? Were they transparent in their relationship with each other, or was everything a pretense? Think about it.

Let me put a definition to our example of fantasy bonding. At first, the definition seems complicated.

Fantasy

Webster's Dictionary definition:

> The power or process of creating especially unrealistic or improbable mental images in response to a psychological need.

In a nutshell, let's say that fantasy bonding would be our unrealistic attachment to an individual or organization, which is in direct response to a need in our lives. If that attachment is ungodly—not ordained by God—it can be an attachment you will one day regret.

Two years from the start of the relationship, our couple is married a year. Because of their consistent pursuit of each other and the time they've invested, they've come to understand that their relationship may have been founded and established on fantasies. They are now tied together, sexually, emotionally, and in their souls. Both are very miserable.

Our soul consists of our mind, will, and emotions. Herein (in our soul) lies the seat of our intellect, our emotions, affections, our feelings, and our passions (desires). When your soul is yoked with someone or some organization, they become an intricate part of your very existence. It can get complicated. Your need to belong and to be a part of them is woven into the fabric of your thoughts.

The Binding Duo

Is there hope for our married couple? Can their marriage be turned around? Are they facing a hopeless situation?

Maybe you're in a similar situation. How did you get to where you are right now?

Can God save their relationship? Of course, God can do anything—but fail. Do they want to save the marriage? Will the young lady and the young man yield to the Spirit of God to save their marriage?

Remember, a tie can be a blessing in a godly relationship, or a thorn in the flesh when you tie up with the wrong person or wrong organization.

More details are needed to adequately assess our couple's relationship. We do know that they yoked up together under false and pretentious circumstances. Neither was ever really honest with the other about who they were and what their expectations were. An unrealistic attachment occurred between them to fulfill a need in each of their lives. You do not want to enter a relationship like that. Marriage is challenging enough without dishonesty in its infancy.

Relationships must be pure and unpolluted by selfishness, manipulation, control, and dishonesty. Love is tantamount to a flourishing, thriving relationship.

Away with abuse in relationships, where one person is always the underdog, controlled and subservient. Such bonding is mere pretense. It's not real, beloved. You deserve better. We've got to love ourselves enough to not allow ourselves to be continually mistreated.

If you're there in the throes of legalism, you can break away, my friend. I know you feel a strong connection to the group. You may even feel you can't make it without them. That's a lie. I know you think you'll be lonely, but loneliness is a choice.

Once you understand fantasy bonding as it relates to abuse, you can make a quality decision to break that bondage of legalism. In Jesus name! Just do it! Do it, and start living again!

Soul Ties

Many people get involved in stale, boring relationships that are not healthy for them. Don't be shocked or surprised at yourself if you've done it too. God help us, though, if we are the type who's prone to continue a pattern of involvement with people and organizations that continually exploit us. Hopefully you're not that type. When you feel you've had all the abuse you can take, you get angry, frustrated, disgusted, and then try to exit the relationship. You try to walk away. But walking away is hard because you've built a tie in your flesh, in your soul—your emotions.

Yes, exiting can be harder than you think. One of the reasons why it can be so hard to dissolve a bad relationship is the connecting link you formed while interrelating and building that friendship. No doubt you formed a bond of kinship and a bond of affection. This link we'll call a tie; and for purposes of breaking the bondage of unhealthy, ungodly, fleshly ties, we'll call them your *soul ties*.

When ungodly soul ties are birthed, over a period of time they become so united that they form a very tight bond—as tight as glue. With such unity comes strength. In this strength an unusual force of power is formed. That's why family and friends who are on the outside looking in, cannot understand the power that holds together that bad relationship. Some of them have asked, "Why don't they just leave?" But this kind of tie has a strange source of strength. Few people can just leave or just walk away. It sounds much easier to do than it really is.

Even after a soul tie is formed and the person finally comes to understand that the relationship is bad for him and he wants it broken, he sometimes finds himself stuck. He'll leave, but run back; leave again, then run back again. The bond is strong, folks, real strong. So if you're trying to leave you must realize that you can't always just walk away. Of course you may not be that person who's trying to leave and can't. Maybe you were strong enough to leave. But hundreds of others out there just can't do it, not without the power of God working in their behalf. This chapter is written to help you see the truth so that you can make a decision to break away from those ungodly ties.

Sometimes you must tear away. Tearing away leaves scars and wounds that take a long time to heal. Keep reading. We'll see this later as we follow the life of Susan, one of our real people discussed in earlier chapters.

What Exactly Is a Soul Tie?

A soul tie is a connection between one person's soul and another person's soul. We must also understand that it can also be a connection between one person's soul and the heart and soul of an organization, a denomination, a group, or any organism. In other words, you can be tied to that organization's founding principles, their vision, their purpose, their popularity, or to their charming charismatic leader.

Some people want to call it commitment, dedication, or devotion. Whatever it is called, if it is an ungodly tie—an ungodly connection, you could actually be building your dedication, your commitment, your devotion on a false foundation. You could be more attached to the creature that was created, than you are to our Creator God.

Or you could be more attached to a man, a woman, an idea, or a cause, than to the most important, powerful force upon which that cause is supposed to be established, God Almighty.

Commitment to God is totally different than commitment to a person, an organization, or a cause. People, organizations, and causes fail us, disappoint us, abandon us, reject us, and sometimes rape us. God never fails. He is faithful. His mercy is from everlasting to everlasting.

People have committed their life's savings, retirement funds, their time, and their lives to television evangelists, ministries, humanitarian groups, or noble causes, only to have been disappointed in the outcome. Many were tied to them because of popularity or because of a need within themselves. When that person or organization's failures became a matter of public record, people were devastated. Many left the church, some even quit God.

We cannot look at the many failures of man. Our eyes must stay focused on Christ. Jesus promised He'd never leave us nor forsake us. When we make Him first priority we are never ashamed. If we get tied to God through His Son Jesus Christ, we're safe and secure for life!

No one should come before our heavenly Father in our personal dedication, commitment, and devotion. He deserves first place in our hearts, in our thoughts, in our pockets, and in our lives. We must put Him there and keep Him there.

If we start our walk with God, let us continue walking with Him. The more we know about Him, the more we need Him in our lives.

Families, churches, corporations, and organizations have split because of a broken tie in its leadership and authority structure.

Consider this scenario; a pastor and his wife have marital problems. Both are prominent, vital, and active authorities in the church which he pastors. Time does not heal their relationship and their marriage breaks up; there is a divorce.

The church family feels the pain and strain of their leaders' split. Unfortunately the congregation chooses sides; some on his side, some on hers.

Some of the members are soul-tied to the pastor. They leave this church and start a new church with him. They vow to follow him wherever he goes. They did not seek God. Those who are soul-tied to the pastor's wife chose to stay.

The presbytery is called in to facilitate. Everybody's affected, everybody's broken. On advice of the presbytery, the wife finds another church to attend. Those who were soul tied to her lost her fellowship. They are weak; they are wounded.

This is not the entire story, but apparently no one really sought God for reconciliation of their leaders. Their flesh ruled.

The pain continues for some time because walking away from a soul tie in the midst of problems is very hard and very painful. This situation would be hard anyway, under any circumstances. Separations and splits of any kind are painful. But had the members been tied first to God, and then demonstrated love and honor for their leaders, God could have sustained them. Pure motives coupled with a sincere prayer life will summon the Holy Spirit in the midst of any situation.

As a rule many people pray what they want, or what their own minds tell them. The burden that the members carried during this unfortunate situation could have been lightened had they sought the mind of God. Their flesh would not have ruled in the gossip. How real is this scenario! They became the talk of the town, and the story changed from mouth to mouth.

Now let's see if we can see the connection between fantasy bonding and soul ties.

Susan's Story: A Victorious Conclusion

In Chapter 10 we read that after leaving her church and seeking the face of God, Susan was delivered from a number of childhood issues that were posing a serious problem in her devotion and in her relationship at her local church. Then we learned that our dear Susan, unaware, went back to that legalistic environment and became even more entangled with bondage. But the Lord was on Susan's side. He is on your side too.

Once again she was faced with pressure, manipulation, and control from spiritual leaders. Susan sought the Lord a second time through fasting and prayer. It was very important for her to hear from the Lord through her ordeal. It should be very important to you as well. This time, during her seeking, the Lord dealt with Susan about her commitment inside the walls of legalism.

Maybe you are inside those same walls trying to find a way of escape and wondering if you're wrong and they're right. Please read the third chapter of Paul's second letter to Timothy. This list strongly identifies some characteristics of ungodly men.

> This know also, that in the last days perilous times shall come. For men shall be
>
> 1. lovers of their own selves,
> 2. covetous,
> 3. boasters,
> 4. proud,
> 5. blasphemers,
> 6. disobedient to parents,
> 7. unthankful,
> 8. unholy,
> 9. Without natural affection,
> 10. trucebreakers,
> 11. false accusers,
> 12. incontinent,
> 13. fierce,
> 14. despisers of those that are good,
> 15. Traitors,
> 16. heady,
> 17. high-minded,
> 18. lovers of pleasures more than lovers of God;
> 19. Having a form of godliness,
> 20. but denying the power thereof;
>
> —2 Timothy 3:1–5

For days and hours upon end Susan found herself meditating on the Word of God, especially the Book of Second Timothy. The Holy Spirit quickened her spirit. The Word of God was illuminating. The Lord began to pour into her His revelation of the characteristics of unfaithful Christians—those who would take advantage of God's beloved. Paul said these were characteristics of people who were ever learning, but never able to come to the knowledge of the truth (2 Tim. 3:7).

Susan's eyes were opened. One by one she examined the list from 2 Timothy 3:1–5. It clearly defined what she had seen, and what she had personally experienced on a regular basis at her church.

As she continued to read the Word of God, the grace and mercy of our loving God was revealed to her as never before. So much of what she received from her Christian leaders at her local fellowship was contrary to the grace and mercy she read about. Instead of grace and mercy she received harsh threats, cruel criticism, demeaning teachings, and an ever increasing push to measure up to an impossible level of their standard of excellence and holiness. God's revealed Word was so unlike what she had been experiencing.

Suddenly she began to look back at the warning signals the Holy Spirit so desperately tried to give her. She thought about how the church leaders constantly pointed out any deficiency they saw in her. Blindly Susan concentrated on pleasing them. If it wasn't pleasing them, she would then concentrate on the error, sin, and the faults they so painfully pointed out. She couldn't comprehend the awesome fact that her sins had been washed away at Calvary. It was wrong for the leaders to put such a yoke of bondage on her shoulders, to undermine Christ's redemptive work. But like so many people, Susan was totally unaware of their tactics. It was a slow process that led her into bondage under their leadership.

But thanks be to God, spurts of freedom now surrounded Susan as she meditated on God's marvelous grace. The more she concentrated on grace, the more legalism was exposed. The Lord started breaking down strongholds and setting her free.

In the Gospel of Matthew, Jesus said that we should take His yoke upon us and learn of Him because His yoke is easy and His burden is light (Matt. 11:28-30). That's exactly what Susan began to do. However, a sorrow came over Susan as she began to realize that so many people in authority have not had the revelation of God's grace. If they had, surely they would not condemn those whom God loves, and for whom Christ died.

How can one who has received and experienced God's grace, deny the same to others? It was a mystery to Susan.

Continuing to read, Susan realized that Paul took time in his letter to Timothy to call the young preacher to be courageous in the faith. In addition, he also took time to remind Timothy about the condition of the world he was living in, and the times that were yet to come. Calling those days *perilous* times, Paul warned Timothy to be aware and to be alert. Harsh, dangerous, fierce, troublesome, and hard to bear times were approaching. Sorrowful characteristics of men and women were gruesomely described. Paul told Timothy he should turn away from those people. Refuse to get involved with them. Don't intermingle with them. They will prove to be detrimental to your life and your walk of faith. The list is very long.

It was almost unthinkable that such attitudes and behavior could be named among those who are of the household of faith, among Christians.

Susan was both saddened and thrilled by these revelations.

Thrilled because finally she understood what she had been going through. Her eyes were now opened to the troubling and continual struggles she had been experiencing as a member of this church. Now she knew it was not all in her mind. It was a great relief. At the same time she was saddened to know that God's leaders are vexing His children and putting a yoke of bondage upon their necks.

Perhaps you are perplexed right now and maybe you, also, are wondering what's right and what's wrong. Certainly what we witness today in some of our churches and among some of our leaders cannot be a true representation of God our heavenly Father.

As Christians have we so misrepresented the Holy One, the Almighty, that true worshipers—people of integrity–are hard to find in leadership today? Can we conclude that most of those we've witnessed and experienced are false teachers, false prophets? Of course not. Are all that we see now lovers of their own selves and lovers of pleasures more than lovers of God? Of course not. The Lord still has plenty of people who have not bowed their knees to legalism.

Inner circles, doctrinal teachers, and leaders are certainly key people who should represent the delegated authority of God in truth and integrity. The Bible requires it of them. We should too.

I can hear some of you saying now, "Don't confuse me with these facts." This is not true of my bishop; not true of my pastor; not true of my overseer. I certainly hope it's not true.

"God forbid that you might be identifying Sister Anointed," one young lady thought. "I just don't believe it." However, this same disbelieving young woman was devastated when she received a harsh rebuke from Sister Anointed. The young lady had genu-inely sought help and understanding on a matter in the church. She spoke with Sister Anointed who had been appointed to assist her. Unfortunately the young lady was slam dunked with more condemnation than she could handle from the leader. She was commanded to repent and submit to all the leadership, and then told that God was displeased that she was questioning authority.

Knowing this kind of situation is true, many of you who are reading this now still find it in yourselves to defend such behavior.

Not able to question? Not able to inquire? Seeking understanding is disrespecting authority? Please, don't insult the intelligence of discerning believers. We are commanded to try the spirit by the Spirit to see if it be of God (1 John 4:1). We come in love and respect to question. We are not to be ignorant. We are not to believe every spirit. Many false prophets are gone out into the world. How many innocent souls have landed under the leadership of one of those false prophets? The scripture did not say a "few" false prophets are out there. It said "many" (1 John 4:1).

Some of you are saying, "I won't believe it." To you I say, go right ahead, my friend. Don't believe what your eyes see, what you heart feels, and what the Spirit is saying to the church. Go ahead, stay in bondage. Don't choose to live a balanced, abundant life.

Susan Continues to Read

"High-minded, high-minded," Susan repeated those words as she thought to herself. She knew that to be high-minded was to have a spirit of pride, to be puffed up with haughtiness and to be conceited (2 Tim. 3:4). This was certainly contrary to the nature of God.

When we think more highly of ourselves than we ought to, and look down our noses at others with contempt, we are very displeasing to the Lord. We shall surely meet with failure.

Since pride goes before destruction, and a haughty spirit before a fall, those afflicted by proud leaders need not lift their voice, nor their hand against them. The Lord will deal with them. Many people have attempted to show them their error, to discuss it scripturally. Most of the time, they're wasting their time. Many of them do not believe anyone is qualified to correct them, question them, or challenge them in the Word.

And anyone who tried to do so met their match in rebuke and reproof. They won't hear it. Proverbs 23:9 says, "Speak not in the ears of a fool: for he will despise the wisdom of thy words."

Day after day as Susan studied and meditated on the Word of God, The Holy Spirit poured into her His desire for her to walk in liberty and freedom under the banner of God's grace. "This is not hard to understand," she kept thinking to herself. "Christians are called to experience an abundant life in Christ. All we need to do is to receive that life, receive what He has already given us—receive it in Jesus' name."

It was all making sense to her now. She prayed:

> Lord I desire to know You. Deliver me from the bondage of legalism. My heart is open, I now receive your abundant life. Your grace is sufficient for me. Fill my heart with more of You.

The Lord heard Susan's cry, and He will hear your cry too. As the Lord continued to reveal the truth to Susan, she was once again faced with a choice—to stay in legalism, or to allow the Lord to lead her out of this bondage for the second time. The choice was an easy one.

The First Time Susan Left

"Why didn't I get it the first time I left this church?" Susan thought. Perhaps the first time the Lord wanted Susan to search her own heart and not point the finger at others. Too many times God's people blame others for their own internal struggles. It's time to stop blaming others for what ails us. It's time to start taking responsibility for ourselves. It's not always someone else's fault. We make some good choices and some bad choices in life. We must face the bad choices in life as well as the good ones. Don't stop to bemoan your bad choice, just pick yourself up, dust yourself off, and allow God to take you into a new area of liberty.

That first time she left her church Susan's heart was honest and her motives were pure. Everything about us may not be spiritually or politically correct, but remember, God looks at our heart, while man is still judging us by our outward actions and appearance (1 Sam. 6:7). Susan had a legitimate concern, and to stay at that time would have been damaging to herself as well as to others. Sometimes we must be led out of one place and into another so that the power of the living God can begin His work within us.

Abruptly leaving your church may not be God's answer for you. Susan sought the Lord. What was right for her may not be right for you. Please do not blindly look for something wrong so that you can leave.

Some people must stay in a certain race in order to win the prize. God has an answer for them which may be totally different from His direction and will for Susan. Some of us must stay planted where He places us until His will is worked out in our lives. Timing is crucial. Obedience is everything.

The first time Susan left her church, although she was hurt and wounded, she still had established soul ties with the leadership and members. Those soul ties were strong, and it was painful for her to leave. Although that church was the source of great pain and agony, it was those same soul ties that beckoned her back into the fold, not understanding that she would continue to experience pain and agony. People will gravitate back to what is familiar, even if the familiar hurts.

So here is the connection, the soul ties drew her back. Relationships had been established and cultivated. Emotional and affectionate ties were formed. Those ties bonded her to the leaders and members of the church. The bonding was ungodly. It was based on a false foundation, not a solid one. It was fantasy bonding—unreal. Real bonding happens when a relationship is established on good solid godly principles. Everybody in the relationship benefits for the good; they thrive, they grow. It's not a one-sided affair. There is no abuse, no condemnation, no fear.

If you're currently in an abusive relationship, seek the Lord. He wants you to be free. No doubt you are also slowly dying inside spiritually. God wants us to serve Him with gladness and in liberty. His grace is amazing.

It was the soul ties and fantasy bonding that caused Susan to return to the same church. She had come to feel better about herself and thought she needed to return to that same fold, so she did. That was all she knew.

The soul ties and fantasy bonding needed to be broken. Susan eventually followed the leading of the Holy Spirit to disconnect herself from this painful abusive union. Remember, your instructions from the Holy Spirit might very well be different from Susan's. Circumstances may be similar, but the situations could be totally different. You must seek the Lord for guidance. He promises to lead and guide you.

Today Susan has relocated to a nearby city where she has found a well-balanced fellowship with loving leaders and loving members. The new church is not perfect, but the leadership allows freedom of thought and the members have a voice, without fear of retaliation and condemnation. All leaders there are expected to be responsible for their own words and actions. They do not charge members with breach of authority or transfer the guilt to them.

The lessons learned are invaluable. Susan is by no means free of problems and concerns. "Many are the afflictions of the righteous: but the Lord delivereth him out of them all" (Ps. 34:19). There is joy in knowing that she can trust God for her future without being under an oppressive bondage of power and control from spiritual leaders.

The joy of the Lord is preeminent and a glow shines forth in her countenance. She is active in her fellowship, and no longer abused. She is better and not bitter. *Balanced*, not bound.

Steps to Susan's Total Victory from Legalism

1. She sought the Lord. She understood that she was not experiencing God's grace, but legalism at her local church. She saw this by the Spirit. She had a revelation of God's grace.

2. She understood that she was being abused spiritually. She made a decision not to be abused any longer. God had something better for her—liberty and freedom in Christ.

3. She stopped resisting and made a decision in her *will* to receive God's grace and to walk in His abundant life.

4. She disconnected herself from that soul tie to which she was falsely bonded.

5. She was delivered once and for all by the power of the Lord. She never returned to bondage again.

6. She walks in freedom and liberty in Christ. The glory of the Lord shines forth in her life.

7. Her life is dedicated to helping others to experience the grace of almighty God. Amen.

CHAPTER 15

LOOK AND LIVE

(WHERE DO WE GO FROM HERE?)

I F YOU'RE READING this chapter, you've come a long way in reading this book. Right about now you might be saying to yourself, "What should I do to get from bondage to balance?"

The four real people discussed in previous chapters—Susan, Barbara, Robert, and Curtis—learned a number of valuable lessons the hard way. It took them time to understand where they were, where they needed to go, and what they needed to do to get there. You'll need to understand these things as well. The steps each of them took were different. One thing they had in common, however, is that they all prayed and sought the Lord.

You must seek the Lord too. You can be sure that God wants to deliver His people from bondage, but the process He wants to use for that deliverance can be quite different from person to person or family to family. What is His process for you? Only He alone can reveal His plan for you as you seek Him through your sincere prayer life. Bondage is not fun and games, it is real and requires a real relationship with Him to get free. It's time to stop name-calling, blaming others, and playing church. Let's get serious, and get free!

It's Not Too Late

Do not think that it is too late for you and your family. It doesn't matter if you have already invested an entire lifetime in the wrong place. It's never too late to look to the future and live. It's not too late to press toward the mark for success and begin to enjoy an abundant life in Christ. Truth is revealed to people at different ages and at different seasons in their lives. The choice is yours; do you want to enjoy the rest of your life free and balanced?

Too many people have decided it's too late for them. They're too old to learn something new. I want to offer this challenge to each of you: decide right now that you're going to enjoy your Christian walk by allowing the Holy Spirit to turn your life completely around. Allow Him to turn your life from bondage to balance. If you yield to the Holy Spirit and let Him lead and guide you, I promise you'll never be the same again. You can't imagine how wonderful life in Christ can be without the bondage, without the control, without the fear, and without the guilt. Start trusting God now; give Him a try. Decide to live. Others have done it. You can do it too!

It Was Not Too Late for Robert;
He Made A Change. God Got the Glory!

In Chapter 12 we revealed that Robert Winters had received a revelation of God's grace. He was delighted. He spent a number of years working in the church to please Christian leaders, thinking this was what God wanted of him. But none of his labor brought him peace or satisfaction. The more he tried to live by the rules set before him, the more he failed. He had grown very weary in his attempts to measure up to what his leaders expected. Guilt ridden and broken inside, Robert looked outside of the Tabernacle and received godly teaching and counsel that ushered him into the very presence of God's grace.

He thought it was too late for him to be happy in church again. Robert's anger and temperament had produced a terrible reputation for him, which led to the loss of respect from Christian leaders and some of the members. But his consistent Bible study habits paid off. The revelation of God's grace through Jesus Christ burst forth in his spirit and set him absolutely free.

He finally realized that the rules he was trying to obey were dictated by the minds of legalists. He could never measure up to what they thought was right for him. He would never be able to please them. Robert made a decision to stop trying to please man by following a set of rules, and to start living under God's grace. What a burden lifted! The guilt fell away. He now understood the error his leaders had made in transferring that guilt to him. His anger subsided and eventually dissipated.

Frustrations now gone, Robert and his family moved their membership from the Tabernacle to another fellowship. It made a tremendous difference in how he viewed himself and others. His family was now happy, because he was at peace. He was able to lead his family to a security in Christ under his restored peaceful leadership.

Serving the Lord freely, Robert continually gives all the glory to the Lord for His power to set his life on the right road. Hopelessness has turned to joy. Today he is elated and *balanced*!

Don't Quit

It was not too late for Robert, and it's not too late for you. You cannot afford to quit now. Please don't even think about never going to another church again. That should not be an option. The Lord's desire is that we would continue coming together to worship and praise. (See Hebrews 10:25.)

There is strength and encouragement when the children of God come together. There is a place just right for you—a place where love abounds and where liberty flows freely in the house of God.

Be steadfast, and always abound in the work of the Lord. He will show you the way. Trust Him.

The Children of Israel Cried Unto the Lord to Free Them From the Taskmasters in Egypt

The Book of Exodus is written to remind us how God rescued His people from the oppression of the Egyptians. We can learn a lot by studying Exodus, but let's try to glean just a few of the great truths found in that book.

The people of God went to Egypt to escape a famine in the land. They were there for hundreds of years. They thrived, grew in population and were treated well because of Joseph, son of Jacob (Gen. 46–48).

After the death of Joseph another king arose in Egypt who didn't know Joseph, and Israel lost the favor they once enjoyed (Exod. 1–9).

Because the people of Israel greatly multiplied in number, the Egyptians became fearful that Israel might side with their enemies in war and defeat them. As a result, the Egyptians forced God's people into slave labor. They set taskmasters (slave bosses) over them to wear them down with hard work.

That's an example of what legalism can do to God's children today. Legalists set themselves as slave bosses over them to manipulate and control them. They wear them down with hard work and make them believe that their slave mentality and subservient attitude towards them is well pleasing to God.

However, we are slaves only to God, not to men. We should be co-laborers in God's vineyard. We submit to God's appointed leaders over us, not with a slave mentality, but as prisoners of Christ. All of us labor together to accomplish God's purpose in the earth today.

God led Israel through generations of slavery in Egypt, but He also made them a great nation of people in the process. When God is in control of your life, He allows you to grow and prosper. That's His pattern.

In addition to the hard labor the Egyptians subjected Israel to, their entire existence was threatened when a death threat was instituted for the midwives to abort all newborn baby boys. It was a very cruel, grievous time for Israel.

Such oppression calls for desperate measures, such as fasting, prayer, and seeking the Lord for deliverance. How desperate are you to be set free? Are you willing to pray, fast, and to cry out to the Lord for your deliverance—for your freedom?

Israel cried out to God to be delivered from their oppressors. God never fails His people. He heard their cry and raised up a deliverer, the man Moses, to bring them out of Egypt. But the process was not a "one, two, three, now you're free" program. The deliverer had a battle on his hands to get God's people free.

Oppressors do not want to let you go. They will lie and tell you that you can leave whenever you want to, just like Pharaoh told Moses. They will make you think that they are not holding you back. But remember, you can be in such fear of leaving that you will stay, because you're made to think that you will die if you do leave. Some people cannot believe that oppressors can have this kind of hold on you, but it's real.

We must be assured that God, our Deliverer, will show us a way out. This book may be just the tool He will use to help.

Leaving One Place and Entering Another

I want to repeat, don't even think about quitting and never going back to any church again. If you listen carefully, the Holy Spirit will lead and guide you to the right place—a place of balance so that your liberty is not compromised with worldliness and sin.

And He brought us out from thence, that He might bring us
in, to give us the land which He sware unto our fathers.
—DEUTERONOMY 6:23

There are many examples of people who have been delivered
from bondage and legalism, but once they were free, they abused
their liberty and freedom in Christ. Here is one incident I'll never
forget.

The Bishop's Wife

A pastor served as bishop over a large denomination in the United
States. The bishop held a prominent position in the organization and his wife was very active and vibrant in ministry as well.
After thirty years of marriage, the bishop passed on and went to
heaven.

After his passing, the bishop's wife walked away from the
denomination, the church, and, many suppose, she walked away
from the Lord too. The last word on her is that she returned to
a worldly lifestyle, which included gambling and frequenting the
horse races, just as she lived before she married the man of God.

Most of you are saying, "Well, she was probably never really
saved." Perhaps not. We don't really know, and it's not ours to
judge. But what we do know is this: when a new kind of freedom
was available to her (singleness because she was now widowed),
she jumped all the way back into worldliness after thirty years of
church service. As believers we are not to love the world, neither
the things that are in the world. If we love the world, the love of the
Father is not in us (1 John 2:15–17).

The conclusion of her story or whether she eventually came
back into the fold is unknown. How sad it is that when her circumstances changed, she changed with them. It's as if she served
alongside her husband only while he served in a position of promi-

nence, but after his death her status as the bishop's wife changed. It was like, "Oh well, now what was I doing?"

Getting the children of Israel to freedom in Canaan was the Lord's doing. First, He had to lead them *out* of Egyptian bondage, before He could bring them *into* the land of freedom in Canaan. It was an *out* and *in* process. You will go through that process too. You will come out before you can go into freedom. It's not always easy. It really is a process. You must face this fact.

The manner in which you leave a place is important. Unfortunately there are times when you will have to tear yourself out and away. Or you may have to run for your life. Other times you can simply walk away and never look back. Every situation is different.

In most instances it is as painful as a divorce. Separation hurts. Everybody is affected, everybody is wounded. You can attempt to get out with grace and dignity, but it is not always possible. Your oppressors will see to it that you are threatened and wounded in the process of exiting, because your leaving speaks about them.

Oppressors will not take it lying down. Pharaoh did not take it lying down either. You can expect harsh words to be exchanged. Pharaoh promised to let Israel go without a problem. It didn't happen. He said they could leave ten times, before the Lord ended it. Remember the plagues.

Before you finally get out, your own behavior might shock you. Then you might even feel guilty at your own responses during the exit. You see, you are very vulnerable and can be easily pulled into a fleshly, defensive, and self-protected interchange of words and accusations.

It isn't necessary to protect yourself, but many people do not know this at the time. Hang in there. Don't take any guilt. The Lord is on your side, just as He was with Israel.

Crossing Your Own Red Sea

And when Pharaoh drew nigh, the children of Israel lifted up
their eyes, and, behold, the Egyptians marched after them;
and they were sore afraid: and the children of Israel cried out
unto the LORD…And Moses said unto the people, Fear ye
not, stand still, and see the salvation of the LORD, which he
will show to you today: for the Egyptians whom ye have seen
today, ye shall see them again no more for ever. The LORD
shall fight for you, and ye shall hold your peace.
—EXODUS 14:10, 13–14

Just like Israel, your transition *out* of bondage can mean that
you will *go through* a season in the wilderness before you cross
over the sea. Fear not, you are waiting for God's total deliverance
out of bondage into freedom and balance. It is a process.

Your Own Wilderness Experience

The wilderness can be a very scary place during transition.
Sometimes you feel lost and abandoned. You're not lost, my friend,
you're certainly not abandoned. During this transition it is crucial
that you seek the Lord. He will lead you into places of revelation,
rest, healing, and learning.

You may find yourself crying a lot. Don't panic, it is a time of
cleansing. Let yourself feel all the pain and hurt that you have gone
through. You're being delivered from the effects of your erroneous
submission. It will be painful—especially when you can still see and
feel the legalists pursuing you. After they left Egypt, Israel looked
up and saw Pharaoh and his armies marching after them too.

It can get very lonely in the wilderness, but remember: God is
with you, and the Holy Spirit is ever present, even if you don't feel
Him. Depend upon Him anyway. What lies ahead is awesome. You
must trust the Lord for that. In fact, try now trusting Him where
you cannot trace Him. Israel wanted to go back to Egypt because

the wilderness was a scary place for them. Bondage in Egypt seemed better to them than to die at the hands of Pharaoh's armies out in the wilderness.

Freedom is always better than bondage. You may still see the enemy coming after you, but open your eyes and also see the Red Sea before you. You'll get there; you'll be crossing over to freedom soon.

The Lord is standing there leading and guiding you. He led Israel by a pillar of cloud during the day and a pillar of fire by night. Trust His leading, despite what you are feeling. Remember, feelings lie to you. You're not alone.

Yes, when Israel saw Pharaoh coming after them, it was a fearful, threatening sight. Suddenly the bondage in Egypt had a certain amount of security in it. They thought to themselves, "At least we were alive. Now we could die in this wilderness." But the Israelites temporarily forgot the severity of the bondage they had left in Egypt. Once you're out, you don't always remember how bad it was when you were in there.

Guard Your Spirit! Forgiveness Is the Key

Remember, during transition you must open your heart for healing of any wounds that you experienced while you were in bondage. When you left you were probably wounded, angry, and possibly bitter. The Scriptures command us to forgive—even our enemies. It may seem hard to do, but with the help of the Holy Spirit, we can forgive. We must forgive! Your deliverance will not be complete unless you forgive.

Wounded spirits must open up and allow God's healing virtue of forgiveness to burst forth within. If you refuse to do so, your entrance into the next place of worship will carry with it bitterness, animosity, hostility, and a bad attitude. Truth will have a hard time penetrating your thought life to affect wholeness inside of you. If you decide not to go to another place of worship, you will still experience a bitter existence.

We must accept the fact that our oppressors may have intended to hurt us, but it was not the will of God, even though they claimed to represent God. The scripture plainly reveals those who are "of" God, and those who are not.

If we refuse to forgive, neither will our heavenly Father forgive us. "Vengeance is mine; I will repay, saith the Lord" (Rom. 12:19). Pray for those who mistreated you and depend on the Lord to deal with them.

Remember, your leaving is not because of something you did, but something they did. Leave them in the hands of a just and righteous God.

Moses, their leader, reminded them that the Lord really was in control. No matter what your eyes see, God is with you. Stand still, Moses proclaimed, and see the awesome salvation of the Lord (Exod. 14:3)! He's working in your behalf. You may see the enemy coming after you now, but the Lord will fight for you if you hold your peace.

Go Forward!

That was God's answer to His people Israel as they cried out again. Right in the middle of their fears, unbelief, and their doubts, the message was: go forward! That is the same word to you, my friend. Go on. Go forward! Freedom is just on the other side as you cross your Red Sea. You will not believe the sweet, awesome lifestyle that awaits you just on the other side—the other side of *through the wilderness.*

Difficulties and trouble during transition are normal. The only way we can get from a place of transition from bondage to a place of freedom and balance is by way of difficulty or crisis.

The Lord's way is the right way. "Better is the end of a thing than the beginning thereof: and the patient in spirit is better than the proud in spirit" (Eccles. 7:8).

Our Savior was also mistreated, but held His peace. In so doing He maintained His power and anointing. I know you don't feel anointed right now. In fact many of you may be wondering now if you really are saved. That is a trick of the devil to convince you that you're not, because of the mixed and manifold feelings you are going through. Don't worry. Some of your current feelings will pass. Press through your feelings. You cannot afford to live by your feelings anyway. The struggle will be over soon and your real feelings will balance themselves out.

I cannot stress enough how important forgiveness is. This transition period is one that can make you or break you. When your spirit is open and you are determined to hold onto an offense, you will let your guard down, then anything is subject to enter in. That's exactly what the devil wants. You can come out of one bondage and enter into another one because your spirit is unguarded, unforgiving. The new bondage, though different, can be as bad, if not worse than the other one.

Make a decision to guard your spirit by yielding to the power of forgiveness with the help of the Holy Spirit. You will not be sorry. In fact you will speed your deliverance. For some people it will take years to overcome bondage, depending upon how deeply they were involved. With others they will come out much faster because they sought the Lord and obeyed His voice.

Be a positive thinker. If you continuously dwell on negative things that happened to you, you will slow down your deliverance. Your wholeness will be based on your positive attitude and your complete trust in the Lord. The Scriptures will be your guide as you begin your steps to healing. Walk in the truth of scripture, not according to your fleshly feelings.

We can overcome any difficulty, trial, or persecution because of Calvary. Jesus overcame the world for us (John 16:33).

While hanging on the cross Jesus prayed, "Father, forgive them; for they know not what they do" (Luke 23:34). His death, resurrection, and forgiveness opened the door for us to enter a relationship with our heavenly Father. Your forgiveness of your oppressors will also open the door for you as you enter new relationships with others. None of your future relationships will be solid unless you forgive.

If you hold onto unforgiveness, people will feel and sense your spirit of anger and bitterness. It oozes out of your pores and out of your mouth; you can't help it. Unforgiveness is a stronghold. Don't be trapped by this ugly spirit. Forgive!

It will be a new day for you, so don't be guilty of sowing the seeds of bad past relationships into new people you meet. Sometimes it seems like it, but everybody is not out to harm you or take advantage of you. God has people of integrity out there. You will meet them if you stay open. Good leaders are ready to sow seeds into your life that will produce good fruit, and you will be thankful to the Lord that you obeyed His command to forgive. Ask the Lord to empty you of any spirit of unforgiveness. Let's do it now.

> *Father, I ask You to help me to forgive anyone who has sinned against me or my loved ones. I want to walk in obedience to Your Word. Cleanse me of all unrighteousness. Create within me a clean heart, a pure heart, so that I can serve You freely. I make a decision now in my will to forgive. With Your help, it is done, right now. Thank You Lord.*

CHAPTER 16

GRACE

I F YOU HAVE been involved in legalism for a long period of time, the clutches of bondage most likely have incarcerated your mind. Most mature people who talk with you can tell. Don't be ashamed. You can be released. Remember the abused, caged mice that were offered their freedom. They went to the door of escape and looked out, but refused to leave their bondage. They were so accustomed to abuse and control that it had become a way of life for them. It will take time for your mind-set to change. Do not look out at freedom and return to bondage because you perceive it to be comfortable and familiar. You may be unacquainted with real freedom, but once you taste it you'll never want to go back to bondage again.

The Opposite of Legalism

Bondage and freedom are opposites. If God delivers you from bondage, as He did the Israelites, you must trust Him to lead you all the way out, and all the way into freedom, or you will lose your balance and go overboard in this newfound liberty. If you don't understand why you came out, you'll go back in after the pain eases up. If you don't know the purpose of your freedom, you will abuse it. Our lives should glorify God.

It is crucial for you to continue to uphold a good Christian moral lifestyle immediately after leaving legalism. Sin awaits you, it lieth continually, at the door (Gen. 4:7). Sin is waiting to attack and to destroy you, but you must rule over it. The temptation to live loosely is ever present, but your love for the Lord should compel you to keep His commandments and walk in holiness.

There is a difference in the holiness taught to you when you were in bondage, and the holiness spoken of in the Word of God. Learn the difference. True holiness is not merely an outward appearance—as some project. Although you have changed your attire and your outward appearance to suit man's definition, true holiness will lead you to an inward sanctification of your heart and life. It is from the inside out that we are to profess His holiness. We consecrate ourselves to live upright and pure before a Holy God, yielding our members daily as we live to represent Him, our Father. Our inward relationship will dictate our outward apparel.

Sanctification: The Principle and Practice of Not Sinning

We cannot afford to lose ground by returning to our old fleshly lifestyle because we were hurt in legalism, or because we think too many limits were attached to our lives. Perhaps that's what the bishop's wife thought—too many rules, too many regulations to follow. Maybe she wanted to go back to having what she remembered as fun. Church people make serving the Lord dull. It is not dull in the least—unless you are bound in legalism.

We must continue on in true holiness by cleansing ourselves of all filthiness of the flesh and spirit, perfecting holiness in the fear of God (2 Cor. 7:1). Determine to live a lifestyle that honors Him.

Curtis' Story: A Final Note of Victory

Curtis Fallbrook found peace and victory when he traded an unbalanced place of worship for a well-balanced one. Although he suffered a little, he was the only one of the four people we previewed who heeded the Holy Spirit's warning before his life was severely damaged.

Curtis did not struggle with what he would do with his life when he left the Mission Church. He did not wrestle with whether to be in the world or in the church. He knew that the Lord had delivered him from the bondage of sin and he was determined to maintain a spirit of thankfulness by serving the Lord with a grateful heart. He had a real conversion experience and understood the sin principle. He did not want to be caught up again in fleshly, carnal things.

As a recipient of God's amazing grace, Curtis has dedicated his life to spreading the good news about grace. His deliverance from the bonds of legalism is a wonderful reminder to all that the Holy Spirit has the power to lead and guide believers into all truth.

Curtis faithfully serves the Lord today and rejoices continually that he is able to come boldly before the throne of grace to receive mercy and to find help in his time of need.

If we, also, are deeply grateful for God's wonderful grace, we should not take advantage of it and live a life displeasing to Him.

Grace Is

1. God's good will and His lovingkindness;

2. God's merciful kindness by which He, exerting His holy influence upon us, turns us to Christ; keeps and strengthens us; increases us in Christian faith, knowledge, affection; and kindles us to exercise all Christian virtues;

3. God's enablement for us to *do* what we cannot do for ourselves;

4. God's enablement to live *for* Him and *in* Him.[1]

Now that you have this enablement to live a holy life, be careful as you enter freedom, that you are not beguiled into a lifestyle that does not honor Him. With all of the rules and regulations from your dictatorial leaders now gone, it is up to you to live upright, by faith, because you love Him and want to keep His commandments. You can now choose to live right—not because a spiritual leader is watching you, but because you know Him and you want, too. To Him be all glory and honor forever. Amen!

You will certainly err at times, but follow God's guidelines for forgiveness when you do sin. In legalism you were made to feel so guilty that you could hardly bear up under the pain of it. That's all gone now. You will miss the mark, but remember not to wallow in sin and lose your anointing. Freedom feels so good, but remember you still belong to a loving God. He still desires a lifestyle that honors Him.

Having freedom now to live by God's wonderful grace can be scary too. You see, you've always had someone telling you that you didn't measure up, that you weren't quite good enough or you have to do it this way or that way. That's all gone now. And, yes, you will question yourself all too often because you're used to reporting in and waiting for instructions, waiting for acceptance and approval. Freedom removes that and allows you to live to please God alone, knowing that in Him you're already accepted in the beloved. Your past, present, and future sins are covered by the blood of Jesus. Christ died once and for all; He does not have to die again.

As you learn to hear the voice of the Lord for yourself, you will find a welcome balance between that which is holy and that which is profane. The Holy Spirit will lead you with His still, small voice. Not a voice of condemnation, but a voice of liberty, freedom, and tenderness. The Holy Spirit is a gentleman. He will not drive you, but He will lead you. You will know and see a difference from the way you were once led by the flesh of legalists, and the way you are now being led by the gentleness of the Holy Spirit. Some make the mistake of going to a new place of balance and dragging the old rules with them, don't you do this!

Abounding in Grace

> What shall we say then? Shall we continue in sin, that grace may abound? God forbid.
>
> —ROMANS 6:1–2

We are no longer servants of sin unto unrighteousness, we must walk like children of light. We are now dead to sin, and have been raised with Christ to live new lives. This is done as we continue to yield ourselves to deeds of righteousness.

Even though we are living under His marvelous grace, we choose not to sin. Should we transgress or sin, we know that Jesus is our advocate. He will intercede for us and plead our case with God our Father. He is with us to help us live successful lives. This freedom and peace we have in Him. It is unbelievable. It is liberating. It is freedom. With this freedom I can now press forward to live a balanced Christian lifestyle.

Many challenges lie ahead of the person who is released from legalism. Victory is on the horizon. Focus on the victory. Don't live in fear, live in victory!

Peter Steps Out of the Boat

For many of you, coming out of legalism will be like Peter stepping out of the boat to walk on the water with Jesus. He was bold and confident until he looked away from Jesus. The disciples saw Jesus walking on the water and thought He was a spirit. Jesus identified Himself and told them not to be afraid. Peter asked the Lord if he could join Him on the water. Jesus said, "Come!" Peter did what no other disciple had done, he walked on the water, just like Jesus (Matt. 14:26–29). You may be the first in your circle to step out in boldness and come out from legalism. Others may follow you if they see that you are successfully out.

Successfully out means you are thriving and balanced; you're not mean, hateful, and bitter. You're a better person, you're full of God's grace. Take care, though, when you step out that you do not take your eyes off the Lord.

Peter took his eyes off Jesus, off the Anointed One, and put them on the boisterous wind. He was frightened of what he saw with his natural eyes. The concentration of Peter's faith was broken because he looked at the circumstances around him (Matt. 14:30).

Once we stop trusting Christ and revert to our natural thoughts—begin reflecting on what we see, what we want; our personal desires, our secret passions, or our own self limitations—we will start to sink like Peter did. Stay focused on the Lord, beloved.

Peter cried out to Jesus to save Him. Jesus saved him, but also reprimanded him by asking him why he doubted (Matt. 14:31).

Fear may grip you too as you step out into new territory, away from the clutches of legalism. Keep your eyes and your focus on Jesus; He won't let you sink. Take one day at a time. Each day you will awaken to new morning mercies. Great is the faithfulness of our loving God. He will not let you down. He will keep you in perfect peace, if you keep your mind stayed on Him (Isa. 26:3).

When God frees His people, He often gives them instructions and warnings before they enter a new phase in their life. Listen for His instructions.

God Instructs Israel After Leaving Egypt

Yes, the Israelites were happy when the Lord delivered them from the hands of the Egyptians, but it wasn't long before they wanted to go back. Having a slave mentality, they did not trust the Lord to lead them all the way into freedom. Remember, it was fear that gripped them when they took their eyes off the Lord and looked at the Egyptians coming after them. (See Exodus 14–20.)

Israel disrespected God and God's delegated authority, the man Moses, on more than one occasion. They did so probably because they were afraid of their current circumstances. Israel would never have disrespected their slave masters in Egypt.

To encourage them, God told Moses to tell His people, Israel, that He was the Lord their God who had brought them out of Egypt, out of the land of slavery. Lest we forget, we too, are His people, and it is He who has delivered us from legalism. We did not deliver ourselves. We must not be haughty or boastful; we must stay humble.

Before Israel could inherit the Promised Land, God gave Moses instructions for His people. We know them as the Ten Commandments. These commandments reveal God's character, His values, and His expectations for His people to function in their relationships with each other. They are timeless truths.

In Exodus 21 God also detailed many other specific laws and instructions for His people. These laws were to protect and provide for them. They also were to be types and shadows which pointed to the coming Messiah promised back in the Garden of Eden.

Christians no longer have to live under certain ceremonial and civil laws given to Moses for God's people to follow. These Old Testament laws pointed to Christ. Legalists, however, have enslaved God's people today by requiring that they keep many of these same civil and ceremonial laws originally intended only for Israel. Although these laws are written for our learning and to help us understand the nature and character of God, many of them were fulfilled in the birth, death, and resurrection of Jesus Christ our Lord. We are not saved by keeping all these laws. Men and women have never had the ability to keep them all anyway, and you can't keep them either.

We Are Saved by Grace

> For by grace are ye saved through faith; and that not of your-
> selves: it is the gift of God: Not of works, lest any man should
> boast. For we are his workmanship, created in Christ Jesus
> unto good works, which God hath before ordained that we
> should walk in them.
>
> —EPHESIANS 2:8–9

Leave it to the devil to complicate God's simple plan of salvation. God gives, man receives. It is God's gift. We cannot earn it.
That's why legalism is so ridiculous. It requires you to work for
salvation, not receive it as a gift. When we try to work for it, we are
always exhausted and disgusted, because we could never achieve
satisfaction. Just about the time we think we have earned it, we
miss the mark again.

It is futile to work for a gift. If you earn it, it is no longer a gift,
but a reward for your labor. Just relax and receive God's grace. It
is God's precious gift. He gave His only begotten Son, Jesus the
Christ. "The law was given by Moses, but grace and truth came by
Jesus Christ" (John 1:17). Amen!

A Call to Embrace GRACE

Throughout the history of man, God has always made provision
to be in relationship with His creation. In the Old Testament God
reveals Himself as a God of *grace* and *mercy* who manifested love
to His people—not because they deserved it, but because of His
own desire to be faithful to the promises made to Abraham, Isaac,
and Jacob.

In the New Testament the theme of *grace* is continued. It is God's
presence and love through Jesus, given to us by the Holy Spirit and
imparting to us mercy, forgiveness, and the desire and power to do
God's will. We are saved by grace, and grace continues to be the

power, presence, and blessing of God experienced by those who receive Christ (Eph. 1:8).

The Lord controls history, judges nations, and delivers people. You're in for a wonderful journey if you choose to live by God's wonderful grace. Welcome! As we see in Scripture and in the world today, we can resist His grace, receive His grace in vain, quench the spirit of His grace, nullify grace, or abandon grace. As you look around the world today, make a decision to choose grace; there is nothing out there that compares, there's nothing better. There are many imitators that offer inner peace through meditation or soul travel, but nothing can duplicate God's grace.

God has made us partakers of His divine nature so embrace His grace. Seek to know Him by an inwrought grace of your soul. Ask Him for the kind of relationship that allows you to accept His deal-ings with you without murmuring, without disputing, and without resisting Him.

The aroma that Christians give off in the world today is to gain the church leader's approval by following a set of rules and regu-lations, thereby thinking to also gain God's approval. Instead we should be wearing a wonderful fragrance of God's grace, whose aroma is a sweet smelling savor to the nostrils of those whose company we are in and a sense of peace to the soul of the person who is troubled.

God Is

Our God is the one and only true God. He has demonstrated His power over all other so-called gods, fashioned in the mind and by the hands of man.

He has looked on the weak, frail, selfish, rebellious nature in man and yet He expresses that He loves us deeply! We have failed Him over and over again with broken vows and broken promises. He, on the other hand, has never failed us for He is long-suffering, patient, and wants us as the apple of His eye—His peculiar treasure.

He has called and appointed flawed people to represent Him before us, His sheep; but will not tolerate anyone continually abusing us, His beloved. He demands obedience of His leaders.

He deals with us in dreams and visions and speaks today through our spirits. He wants us to focus on His Word and get to know Him as Creator and Redeemer. In really *knowing Him* we will desire to worship *Him* only, and to wholly become *His* people.

Our God is holy, faithful, compassionate, loving, marvelous, and mighty.

He wants us to sacrifice our lives to Him—not to control us, but so that He may shepherd and guide our lives, and to convey unto us a *balanced abundant* existence on earth.

God is a covenant keeping God, and Jesus is still Lord of all! He is the "I AM that I AM" (Exod. 3:14)! He is more than enough, and His Grace is sufficient for us all! Amen!

RESOURCES AND RECOMMENDED READING

Cloud, Henry and John Townsend. *Boundaries in Marriage.* Grand Rapids: Zondervan Publishing House, 1999.

Enroth, Ronald M. *Churches That Abuse.* Grand Rapids: Zondervan Publishing House, 1992.

Enroth, Ronald M. *Recovering From Churches That Abuse.* Grand Rapids: Zondervan Publishing House, 1994.

Nelson, Thomas. *Nelson's Electronic Bible Reference Library.* Nashville: Nelson Electronic Publishing, 2000.

Spurgeon, Charles. *Grace, God's Unmerited Favor.* New Kensington: Whitaker House, 2003.

Swindoll, Charles. *The Grace Awakening.* Nashville: Thomas Nelson Publishers, 2000.

Wiersbe, Warren. *Be Free: Galatians.* Colorado Springs: Cook Communications, 1975.

www.info@cultclinic.org. New York: Cult Hotline and Clinic, 1980.

Yancy, Phillip. *What's So Amazing About Grace.* Grand Rapids: Zondervan Publishing House, 2000.

The Holy Bible, New Living Translation. Wheaton, IL: Tyndale House Publishers, Inc., 2004.

NOTES

Preface

1. Cultclinic.org, "Cult Statistics", http://cultclinic.org/qa2.html (accessed February 12, 2007).

Chapter 3
Heaven's Weights and Measures

1. Rufus McDaniel and Charles H. Gabriel, "Jesus Came into My Heart," 1914.

Chapter 4
The Fountain of Life

1. William Cowper, "There is a Fountain Filled with Blood," 1772.

Chapter 5
A Balanced Look at Biblical
Qualifications for Leadership

1. *Matthew Henry's Commentary on the Bible*, Nelson's Electronic Bible Reference Library (Nashville, TN: Thomas Nelson, Inc., 1997).
2. "The Peoples Temple Church," http://religiousmovements.lib. virginia.edu/nrms/Jonestwn.html (accessed May 7, 2007).
3. "Branch Davidians," Rick A. Ross Institute, http://www.rickross. com/groups/waco.html (accessed February 7, 2007).
4. "Heavens Gate," http://en.wikipedia.org/wiki/Heaven%27s_Gate_ %28cult%29 (accessed March 6, 2007).

Chapter 6
Looking Back to Today

1. *The Godfather,* Internet movie database, http://www.imdb.com/title/tt0068646/ (accessed February 7, 2007).

Chapter 8
The Vulnerable and Innocent

1. "The Branch Davidians," Rick A. Ross Insitute, http://www.rickross.com/groups/waco.html (accessed February 7, 2007).

Chapter 16
Grace

1. *Matthew Henry's Commentary on the Bible.*

TO CONTACT
THE AUTHOR

Wondrous Grace Ministries
P.O. Box 543
Florissant, MO 63032

Phone: (314) 355-0212
FAX: (314) 741-8759
E-mail: wgministry@aol.com